KNOWING THE SCORE

KNOWING THE SCORE

The Past, Present and Future of Cricket Scoring

Keith Booth

Foreword by Bill Frindall

MAINSTREAM
PUBLISHING

EDINBURGH AND LONDON

First published in Great Britain in 1999 by
MAINSTREAM PUBLISHING COMPANY (EDINBURGH) LTD
7 Albany Street
Edinburgh EH1 3UG

ISBN 1 84018 197 4

A catalogue record for this book is available from the British Library

Typeset in Garamond
Printed and bound in Great Britain by Biddles Ltd

Contents

With his roots in the same Barnsley soil as Geoffrey Boycott, Dickie Bird and Michael Parkinson, Keith Booth has inherited a love of cricket which has stayed with him all his life.

Now with Surrey, he is well established in his second career as a cricket scorer and author. He has previously worked with Middlesex and MCC and was scorer to the BBC's *Test Match Special* team in the West Indies in 1994. He is the author of *Atherton's Progress*, and this is his second cricket book.

Keith is married with two grown-up daughters and lives in Sutton with his wife Jennifer who is Archivist of the Tate Gallery, and Surrey's reserve scorer. When his scoring commitments permit, he still plays club cricket and such residual time as he has is devoted to his stamp collection and running the occasional marathon.

Acknowledgements

This book would have been impossible without the support and assistance of numerous people and organisations. My sincere and heartfelt thanks are particularly due to the following:

Public Record Office
Hampshire County Record Office
Centre for Kentish Studies
Surrey County Record Office
Public Libraries of Mitcham, Sevenoaks, Upper Norwood and Harlow
P A Sport
United Distillers for information on the 'Johnnie Walker' Scoreboards
Tate Gallery
Frikkie Botha, Designer of 'Cricket Wizard'
Theo Braganza, Secretary, and Dr Vasant Naik, Vice-President, Association of Cricket Scorers and Statisticians of India
Dr J.S. Briggs, formerly of the Department of Computer Science, University of York
Marion Collin, Archivist, Women's Cricket Association
Stephen Green, Curator, MCC Museum
Jeff Hancock, Librarian, Surrey County Cricket Club
Brian Hughes, New South Wales Cricket Association
Abid Ali Kaz, Pakistan Association of Cricket Statisticians
Michael Meredith, Librarian, Eton College
Ross Peacock, Librarian, Melbourne Cricket Club
Jena Pullman and Christine Thornton, Melbourne Cricket Club
Robert Sackville West and the Trustees of Knole Estates
SLR Cricket Company
R.D. Thomas, Secretary, Sevenoaks Vine Cricket Club
O.H. Whittaker, Registrar, Worshipful Company of Stationers and Newspaper Makers
Mike Ringham, scorer to Australian touring teams of 1977, 1981 and 1985
The late John Featherstone, Yorkshire County Cricket Club
Gordon Vince for information on his Cricket Statistics System
Bernard Whimpress, Curator, Adelaide Oval Museum
All scorers on the county circuit for their bonhomie and sharing their wealth of experience

Finally, special thanks are due to Bill Frindall for finding time in a busy schedule to write the Foreword, to my wife Jennifer for her invaluable assistance with indexing and proof-checking, and to our cat Polly for regularly rearranging the many piles of information from which the book has been compiled.

Keith Booth

Foreword

By Bill Frindall

It is both an honour and a delight to be invited to contribute a foreword to Keith Booth's illuminating survey of all aspects of cricket scoring and its associated trappings. In a comparatively short time, Keith has become a highly respected scorer at international and county level. He is unique in having recorded Test matches both as the official England scorer at The Oval and as the BBC Radio *Test Match Special* scorer/statistician on an entire tour of the Caribbean.

Knowing the Score is far more than the history of cricket scoring which I had expected. After delving into every facet of scoring's development from the earliest notches to the latest laptop technology, it deals with scorecards, scoreboards and statistics. His chapter on 'Politics and Administration' includes an authoritative but sensitive survey of the 1997 skirmish between county scorers and the England & Wales Cricket Board in which strike action was threatened but swiftly abandoned. The following year county scorers were again the hapless victims of incredibly inept scoring software which has been outrageously foisted upon them at short notice and after inadequate testing. More militant artisans would have downed tools and deserted their posts. These are men who do the job because they love cricket and for whom the payment, often derisory and in the case of two counties merely basic expenses, is irrelevant. It is high time that they were credited alongside the umpires in *Wisden Cricketers' Almanack* and included with umpires and groundsmen in the presentations of medals which conclude major international matches and Lord's finals.

As one who, when aged ten, was taught to score by a desperate novice teacher on a rainy sports afternoon four days before deputising for an absent official at my local club, I count myself exceptionally fortunate to have been associated with scoring for 50 summers, the last 33 on a professional basis. As this book shows, scoring has rather lagged behind other cricket techniques in its rate of development. Although Bill Ferguson devised the linear system in 1905, on the first of his 42 tours around the world, it was not until 1966, when I revised the system and began marketing scoresheets, that scorers began assessing the duration of a batsman's innings in terms of balls rather than minutes. It took several more years to persuade administrators and sponsors that awards for fastest 50s and 100s should be assessed by fewest balls faced. Incidentally, it was one of Keith's predecessors as Surrey scorer, Jack Hill, who first used my scoresheets at first-class level in 1971.

Bill Ferguson was a remarkable man who gained his introduction to international scoring by 'chatting up' his dentist. The latter happened to be one of Australia's greatest all-rounders, Monty Noble. As a truant schoolboy, I had the pleasure of meeting 'Fergie' during a Kingston festival match in 1953. A tiny man in a trilby hat, he showed me his scorebook during the tea interval. Besides recording the match in the official book and keeping his private linear sheets, he found time to produce his famous radial scoring charts (also conceived in 1905) and sketch features of the ground in the margins of the scorebook. In addition, he was responsible for every item of the touring team's vast baggage and never mislaid one. All students of scoring should read his autobiography, *Mr Cricket*, published shortly before his death in 1957.

Perhaps the most surprising aspect of this volume is that it is the first comprehensive chronicle on the subject. It will fascinate all cricket-lovers, particularly those who have ever operated a scorebook, however unwillingly.

Bill Frindall
Urchfont, Wiltshire

Chapter One

Notchers and Early Records

Throughout history, sport has reflected the nature of the society that has produced it. The pentathlon of ancient Greece, comprising running, jumping, wrestling, throwing the discus and the javelin, echoes the military nature of the city states. Two and a half millennia later the divergence between rugby league and rugby union in 1895 epitomises the class distinctions of Victorian England, and a century beyond that the reconciliation of the two codes comes at a time when those distinctions, if not eliminated, have certainly become more blurred. Likewise, the professionalisation, sponsorship and media buy-

'An Exact Representation of the Game of Cricket' (c1760 – W.R. Coates after L.P. Boitard) showing the notchers on their low mound (parvo in colle) at mid-wicket [Tate Gallery]

outs of not only rugby union, but association football, tennis and the Olympic Games coincide with a general commercialisation of life, the rise of marketing as a major business discipline and the emergence of a generation of couch potatoes addicted to watching sport on the telly.

Cricket is not exempt from this general pattern; indeed, it is, possibly more than any other sport, a microcosm of social history: aristocrat and journeyman, master and servant, gentlemen and player, professional and amateur co-exist, often uneasily, until in 1962, the distinction is abolished and all become 'cricketers'. Neville Cardus, who took the view that 'cricket holds up the mirror to the English nature' (1) might not recognise the game that is played today and today's players might not recognise the game loved by Cardus. But it still reflects nature and society and not only English nature and society. The development of the game in the Caribbean cannot be divorced from rising nationalism and independence movements (2) and in the days of the British Empire, cricket was seen as a medium via which the colonials could cock a snook at the mother country. But like society, the game becomes professionalised and commercialised, more classless, more prone to market forces.

Even so, changes have not been without their detractors. Four years before the demolition of the glass ceiling separating the Gentlemen from the Players, an MCC Committee comprising inter alia a duke, two colonels, a reverend and no one with fewer than two initials, had 'rejected any solution to the problem on the lines of abolishing the distinction between Amateur and Professional and regarding them all alike as "cricketers"' and the editor of *Wisden* in his annual notes laments the change:

> 'By doing away with the amateur, cricket is in danger of losing the spirit of freedom and gaiety which the best amateur players brought to the game.' (3)

Inevitably, the history of cricket scoring must reflect the history of the development of the game itself and while the parallel will not be absolutely exact, it is interesting that scoring – and indeed ancillary areas such as scoreboards, scorecards and statistics – has reflected the presupposed superiority of the batsman (the aristocrat, the amateur, the gentleman) over the bowler (the journeyman, the professional, the player) whose function is to put the ball into play to be hit. The contrast is perhaps more marked in the West Indies where until the 1920s, the white men, who can afford the equipment, are batsmen; the black men, who cannot, are the bowlers. (4) Even today, where traces of the former order survive – MCC, public school and fancy hat sides – one hears talk of 'declaration cricket', as though the option of bowling out the opposition were not open to the fielding side.

The batsman–bowler relationship in the eighteenth and nineteenth centuries was very much master and servant, aristocrat and minion. Professional cricketers were employed as 'bowlers' by county clubs. In 1846, the era of the professional touring XIs had not yet arrived and the stark class distinctions of the period percolate the minutes of the establishment at play, the Marylebone Cricket Club:

> ... complaints having been made that the Bowlers of the Club are not always in the way when wanted, more especially when a match terminates on a practice day.

> Leave of absence during the Week will not be granted to any Bowler who shall not have signalled his wish to the Hon Secretary, or a member of the Committee, if on the ground, before Three O'clock on Monday.

> No bowler, unless employed on the Service of the Club, will be allowed to be absent more than four practice days during the Season and then efficient substitutes must be found.

> At the conclusion of a match half an hour will be granted to the Bowlers who have either played, scored, or stood Umpire; and at the expiration of that time they must take their places on the ground, the others must have the wickets pitched for practice. (5)

And so, in the history of recording the game, batsmen's scores are listed some time before bowlers are credited with wickets taken, batting averages chronologically precede bowling averages, scorecards do not always recognise that the professionals too might have initials and, at least in England, it is only the most detailed scoreboards that include bowling figures. Individual batsmen's totals have been displayed since the late nineteenth century.

Maybe it is logical that batting records and statistics take precedence over and precede chronologically those relating to bowling; maybe it is just coincidence and does not reflect any perceived superiority of the art of batting over that of bowling: but, by contrast, in the less class-ridden USA, the boxscore system, introduced by Henry Chadwick in the 1850s, gives batter's and pitcher's statistics equal prominence. (6)

The origins of cricket are lost in obscurity and outside the scope of this study, but the likelihood is that it emerged from the Dark Ages as a rural pastime for shepherds before being taken over by the gentry and aristocracy, partly for entertainment and recreational purposes but largely as a vehicle for gambling. The records of the Hambledon Club, long revered as the cradle of the modern game, indicate that it was basically a gentlemen's drinking club for which cricket and betting were annexed for the entertainment of the members.

Christopher Brookes identifies five distinct phases of the English game:

1. The age of the folk-game *(pre-1660)*
2. The era of the aristocracy and gentry *(c 1660–1830)*
3. The era of the professional XIs *(c 1830–1870)*
4. The apogee of amateurism *(c 1870–1945)*
5. The business years *(post-1945)*. (7)

By the eighteenth century, it had become competitive and as inextricably linked with betting as horse-racing is today. The first *Laws of the Noble Game of Cricket* (1744) contain a section on gambling and by 1788 there is a quite logical prohibition on gambling by players and umpires, but interestingly not by scorers. Whether this omission is a reflection of scorers' integrity or their insignificance is unclear. Notwithstanding that, it was essential to have an accurate record of the scores and the function of the photofinish camera was undertaken by the scorer.

Scoring develops alongside the game itself and, as well as reflecting class divisions, broadly follows these developments, having three separate but chronologically overlapping incarnations, each more sophisticated than its predecessor, as data is recorded in the eighteenth century on wooden sticks, in the nineteenth century on paper and in the late twentieth, on computers.

At the time of the folk-game, there was little need to keep the score – or, at least, to keep it accurately: it is questionable whether any were kept and fairly certain that none have survived. It is the hi-jacking of the game by the aristocracy and its use for gambling purposes that leads to the necessity for records to be kept. There was now a need for the score to be known so that wagers could be settled and scorers began to appear not from the woodwork but with it. The records they kept became more sophisticated over time until the IT explosion of the late twentieth century caused the game and its scoring systems once again to be invaded by commercial interests and the placid, rarely disturbed world of the County scorebox to be invaded by laptops, printers, monitors and all the paraphernalia of computerisation, the impedimenta of a media-driven desire for more and more statistical information.

The word *score* as a noun and transitive or intransitive verb had originally nothing to do with keeping a numerical record. Its etymological origins can be found in the Old English *scoru* and Old Norse *skor* which mean simply to make a notch or a mark as in 'score along the dotted line'. It is only by extension that it comes to have anything to do with counting and does so because of the method of 'scoring' notches on sticks.

Such a method of counting, precedes and is by no means peculiar to cricket scoring. In the late fifteenth century, it was in use as part of the 'tally' system, an antecedent of both carbon paper and the credit card.

Tallies were wooden sticks, notched to represent a given sum and split, the Exchequer retaining one half by way of record. The other half could either be used in the process of accounting, as a receipt for money paid in, or as a 'tally of assignment' authorising payment of royal money by a specified collector of revenue who would later produce the tally to prove his payment. (8)

Rev. James Pycroft in his great mid-nineteenth-century treatise on the game *The Cricket Field* refers to a sturdy yeoman cutting notches with his bread-and-bacon knife on an ashen stick and Ashley-Cooper's edited version traces the custom back even further, adding in a footnote:

When the runs were notched on a stick, every tenth run was cut deeper so that the whole could be counted more expeditiously (Debts used to be recorded by notches cut in a tally-stick, and so ancient was the custom that such sticks have been found in the Aquitaine caves of Périgord in Southern France). (9)

The use of score to mean twenty as in the psalmist's threescore years and ten, is, the *Shorter Oxford Dictionary* suggests, of Icelandic origin and passes into English from the custom of counting sheep orally from one to twenty and marking a 'score' or notch on a stick before proceeding to the next twenty. It is probable therefore that this primitive method of recording leads to 'score' coming to mean 20.

Similarly, the origins of cricket 'scoring' can be traced to the carving of notches on hazel sticks, but sheep tend to move at a greater pace than that at which runs are accumulated and there is time for the scorer to carve a notch for each run with perhaps a larger notch for the twentieth and subsequently for the fifth, tenth, fifteenth etc. The margin of victory or defeat in early matches is usually expressed in notches. There are exceptions, however. The 1744 Laws provide that 'Each Umpire is ye Sole Judge of all ... good or bad Runs at his own wicket' and the term 'run' is used occasionally thereafter, for example:

And underneath the shady tree
The Scorer's [sic] fix'd the Runs to see. (10)

17

It was not, however, in general use as a performance indicator until about 1800 and the 1809 version of the 'Laws as revised by the Club at St Mary-le-bone' still provides that 'If the Striker runs a short Notch, the Umpire must call "No Notch"'. As late as the 1820 version the Laws are still referring to notches. (11)

'Notch' first appears in English in 1577 and three years later is used to indicate a nick made on a stick etc. as a means of keeping a score or record. That meaning is easily and naturally absorbed into cricketing vocabulary a century or so later.

The earliest known description of a game is in a Latin poem of 1706 by William Goldwin, an old Etonian and scholar of King's College, Cambridge. The poem, *In certamen Pilae, Anglice, A Cricket Match* – literally, To the Ball Game! – was translated in 1922 by H.A. Perry and the scorers – or notchers as they then were – receive due recognition:

> on a low mound, whence clear the view,
> repose a trusty pair and true:
> their simple task with ready blade,
> notches to cut, as runs are made

An alternative translation by P.F. Thomas appears the following year in *Early Cricket*:

> Two trusted friends squat on the rising floor
> To notch, with knives on sticks, the mounting score (12)

Both are clearly loose paraphrases rather than accurate translations of the original Vergilian hexameter:

> Parte alia, visus qua libera copia detur,
> Parvo in colle sedent duo pectora fida, parata
> Cultellis numerum crescentem incidere ligno.

which might, more accurately but less poetically, be rendered:

In another place, from where the view is abundantly clear, two faithful souls sit on a small hill, ready with little knives to cut the growing number on the wood.

Both Perry and Thomas translate as 'notch' the original 'incidere' and the use of 'run' is clearly an anachronistic superimposition of the early twentieth century on the early eighteenth. In fairness, however, it must be said that the term 'cursus' is used in the immediately preceding lines which deal with the umpires:

> Stant Moderatores bini stationibus aptis
> Fustibus innixi, quos certo attingere pulsu
> Lex jubet, aut operam cursus perdemus inanem.

rendered by Perry as:

> Each at his wicket, near at hand,
> propped on his staff, the Umpires stand,
> the runner's bat must touch their pale,
> or else the run will nought avail.

The likelihood is then that both 'notch' and 'run' are used through the eighteenth century with the former dominating, until the notchers are superseded by the paper and pencil merchants in the nineteenth. As an aside, however, it is perhaps illuminating that our trusty souls are given a 'visus ... libera copia', an abundantly clear view, a circumstance not always replicated some three hundred years later, even on Test match grounds.

A piece of eighteenth-century doggerel, contemporary with Swift and Pope, though scarcely comparable in quality, informs us that:

> His Grace the Duke of Dorset came
> The next enrolled in skilful fame
> Equalled by few, he plays with glee
> Nor peevish seeks for victory
> And far unlike the modern way
> Of blocking every ball at play
> He firmly stands with bat upright
> And strikes with his athletic might
> Sends forth the ball across the mead
> And scores six notches for the deed. (13)

The six notches would be 'all run', the 'boundary six' being unknown before 1910, but, whatever its literary merits, the piece does serve to indicate that the standard unit of cricket measurement in the eighteenth century was the notch not the run.

Further evidence is provided in the *Order Book* of the Hambledon Club where on Tuesday, 4 May 1779 it is 'orderd':

that the Names of Members that attend each day shall be inserted in a Book to be kept for ye Purpose together with the Names of the Players and Number of Notches gott by each.

Not only an indication of the method of scoring, but also perhaps the first reference to the collection of statistics referring to individuals as distinct from those relating to matches.

A painting of a cricket match, possibly by W.R. Coates, but certainly derived from an engraving by H. Roberts after L.P. Boitard, little more than a generation later than Goldwin's poem, confirms the presence and location of the notchers on their low mound, though strategically placed at mid-wicket, well within the playing area.

In the Memorial Gallery at Lord's hangs a well-known painting entitled *The Game of Cricket as played in the Artillery Ground, London 1743*, once assumed to be by Francis Hayman, but now attributed by those who know something about art history to an unknown copyist after C. Benoist (after Hayman) (14), which shows batsman and underarm bowler in serious confrontation, fielders and umpires paying minimal attention, but the scorer wrapt in concentration. The main difference from his twentieth-century counterpart is that he has a stick and sharp knife, but there are also major variations from his predecessors in the Goldwin poem (1706) and his contemporaries in the Coates painting (1743–5 according to Robin Simon and Alastair Smart in their *Art of Cricket*, although the Tate Gallery says 1760) in that he is alone and is strategically placed at silly mid-off! It is possible that the different position and the fact that there is just one notcher and not two reflects a fundamental difference in the nature of the games depicted, the one we have on the anonymous painting being very clearly a single-wicket match, while the one to which the poem and Coates painting relates is the double-wicket version of the game.

More information would be required before firm conclusions could be drawn, but the evidence points towards the notchers already being an important and integral part of the game, operating in pairs at mid-wicket during double-wicket matches and solo at silly mid-off in single-wicket encounters. A novel method of keeping track of the progress of a match preceded written records in the West Indies. Apparently, leaves were placed in a hat, one leaf for every run scored, in the first innings and then removed at the rate of one leaf for every run scored in the second innings. If the hat had been emptied before the team batting second were dismissed they had won, but if there were still leaves in the hat when the last wicket fell, they had lost by whatever the number of leaves remaining.

There is no fixed point at which notching ceased and recording the score on paper took over: indeed the evidence suggests that the two methods co-existed throughout the latter half of the eighteenth century and a brief article in *The Cricketer* by F.G. Forman on 25 July 1953 suggests that the notching method was in use in Derbyshire as late as the end of the nineteenth century.

The nearest I have come to anything approaching notching in the twentieth century is a scoring device with a resemblance to a cribbage board where pegs are placed in three rows of holes numbered 0 to 9, 10 to 90 and 100 to 500. It is notching only to the extent that it is a non-paper record and the 'notches' are pre-prepared. It was the property of the Somerset Stragglers Cricket Club and presented to the County Club in 1933. Presumably it had not been used for some time before that.

Rowland Bowen's reference to the emergence of written records points to both notching and written records operating simultaneously and gives an early example of the way in which 'unofficial' scoring led by the media's requirement for more detailed information has been in advance of 'official' scoring, the function of which is to provide basic information on the state of the game at the time.

> ... the full stroke-by-stroke score was kept of the Duke of Dorset's team and was obviously being kept long before it looked as though Minshull was going to establish any kind of record. What then can be the meaning of those old paintings of men sitting halfway to the wicket cutting notches into staves found for many years after 1769 if, by that date and by inference therefore much earlier 'scoring' as notch-cutting was called had been reduced to pen and paper? It cannot merely be poetic licence because the Kent v Hampshire match of July 8-9 1783 was first reckoned to have been a tie because the scorers had made an error – one of them, Pratt, produced his stick as evidence that he had made a mistake in cutting the eleventh, instead of the tenth longer than the others...

> It seems that the old method of 'scoring' continued in existence, perhaps to provide the 'official' tally of the final totals, though the details had for many years been committed, perhaps less accurately, to paper. If so, it is another example of the way 'scoring' in cricket has remained officially well behind unofficial scoring: even now, the official scorers keep an inadequate detail of what goes on in a match and it has to be contrasted with the wealth of data maintained by the Press or wireless statisticians, where one may find out how many balls were bowled by each bowler to each batsman and many other far from negligible items. (15)

Apart from their representation in painting and poetry, there is not too much information on early scorers and most remain anonymous. One exception is T. Pratt mentioned here by Bowen. He was scorer to the Vine Club, Sevenoaks, and represents perhaps an important link between notching and scoring on paper. He was a printer who in 1773 produced the earliest surviving scorecard of a Grand Match on Sevenoaks Vine, Hambledon Club with Yalden against England.

It is unclear whether Pratt maintained any scoresheets or scorebooks. There are certainly none extant and it may well be that he continued as a notcher and produced scores retrospectively from his notes and/or memory. His significance, however, lies in the fact that he combined his profession as a printer and his hobby as a scorer to record some statistical detail of matches for posterity. Gerald Brodribb records that a card of a later match shows a lunch-time score 'with the state of the game' (16) – a practice not much in evidence some two hundred years down the road!

It is known that the same T. Pratt was responsible for the printing of the scores of most of the matches of the Hambledon Club from 1777–88 and advertised in a Kent newspaper in 1776 'a correct list of the ensuing game at Sevenoaks' (between the Hambledon Club and Kent) 'within half an hour after the game was finished.' (17)

The earliest match where the batsmen's individual scores are recorded was played at the Artillery Ground on 2 June 1744, but the match played a little later, on 18 June, between Kent and All England is historically more significant. Not only are individual scores recorded, but also how the batsmen were dismissed and by whom – though at this stage in cricket history, bowlers receive no credit for catches taken from their bowling and the recording of actual bowling figures is still some one hundred years away.

The likelihood is however that the match was recorded by an anonymous journalist rather than the official scorer-notcher and it is here that we have perhaps the first divergence between the immediacy of 'official' scoring for the players and spectators at the time and 'unofficial' scoring for the benefit of the media and the public. The former seems to remain static while the latter is developed via Pratt and others and later becomes more sophisticated as the game itself becomes more organised and codified, with the establishment in 1787 of the successor to the White Conduit Club, the MCC, which was to begin the process of developing in the world of cricket a position of pre-eminence that was to endure for a further two centuries. The Club had an official scorer in Samuel Britcher.

Not a great deal is known about him beyond a brief note in A.D. Taylor's *Annals of Lord's and History of the MCC*. Published in 1903, with a description on the fly-leaf that typifies the verbal incontinence of much writing at the turn of the century, 'A concise record of the Club's progress gleaned from authentic sources from the date of its foundation to the present time' this brief history informs us that:

> ... the Marylebone Club had a regular scorer in Samuel Britcher – a highly educated individual, who ignored the old method for the pencil. He held his position at Lord's for a number of years, and in 1802 published a book of scores ranging from the year 1793 to 1802."

There has, however, been some recent research into his family background by Patricia Roberts, and David Rayvern Allen ran an interesting series of articles, 'Samuel Britcher, the hidden scorer', in *The Journal of the Cricket Society* in autumn 1980, spring and autumn 1981.

In 1790 Britcher produced a *List of all the Principal Matches of Cricket* with a correct state of each innings. Before that, however, he had published annual lists of matches and it was in 1793 (the fact that the reign of terror was in full swing across the Channel is, one assumes, nothing more than coincidence) that a final page of aggregates and averages was added and the concept of the batting average was born. The series continued until 1805. They were not scorebooks as such and indeed, the range of matches covered makes it highly unlikely that Britcher would have attended them all, but rather collected scores from accomplices or fellow enthusiasts. In 1823, Henry Bentley produced something more comprehensive, which was later to be an inspiration to the spirit of enquiry of Arthur Haygarth, namely *A Correct Account of All the Cricket Matches Which Have been Played by the Mary-le-bone Club and all the Principal Matches from the Year 1786 to 1822 Inclusive*. These too were *ex post facto* records, rather than scorebooks, and the importance of the work of both Britcher and Bentley lies in their being the first work of statistical record and the antecedents of Lillywhite's *Scores and Biographies of Celebrated Cricketers* and 136 editions (to 1999) of *Wisden Cricketers' Almanack*.

The Centenary Edition of the latter (1963) contains a fascinating section on Dates in Cricket History by H.S. Altham where the first reference to cricket is traced to the wardrobe accounts of Edward I in 1300. There are then intermittent references which become more regular in the seventeenth century. The first indications of the existence of any formal keeping of the score is, as indicated above, 1744 with the preservation of what is referred to as the full score (certainly as full as anything at the time, though, less full than records subsequently became) of the 'great match' between Kent and All England played on the Artillery Ground at Finsbury. It was in this year that the Laws of Cricket were first codified and it is clear that the game was now moving from an informal pastime to one with something of a semi-formal and organised structure. It is from this point that the history of scoring is closely parallel to the history of cricket and its laws.

In 1751, according to Altham's list, the first refinement is added to score-keeping in that the score at the fall of each wicket is recorded and, although there was provision for this on nineteenth-century scoresheets, it is perhaps salutary to note that 200 years elapsed since its introduction before the practice became standard in *Wisden*.

The year 1777 saw the first instance of a bowler being credited with catches taken from his bowling and in 1836 the bowler was first credited by name with catches and stumpings. The emphasis remained, however, very much on batting: as we have seen, the concept of the batting average had developed by the end of the century, but the first example of bowling analysis in the form familiar to us today appeared in the same year as the penny post, 1840. Some thirty years later, the advice on the title page of the 20 shillings *Cricket Scoring Book for 450 Matches* published by Bell's Life in London is 'To find out your best bowlers it is requisite that you should analyze the bowling yearly and average the runs obtained from each over.' The general use of average runs per wicket came later still.

Alfred D. Taylor in his book mentioned above records that:

About 1840 the bowlers analysis commenced to be recorded in the M.C.C. scoring book, though only at irregular intervals; indeed, it was many years later before the rule was universally recognised. The introduction is believed to have been the result of a proposition suggested by George Lee, the umpire and brother to Harry Lee, the celebrated cricket reporter at Lord's at that period.

Crediting bowlers with wickets taken was in fact slowly absorbed into scoring traditions and seems only gradually to have become the norm. Around 1850, Lillywhite writes:

This was a vast improvement in recording the game, and but justice to the bowler. Many of the bowlers of early days, including Lumpy, Harris, Beauclerk, Wells, Budd, Hammond...etc have many wickets lost to them owing to this omission, and many of their feats deteriorated in consequence.

It is an astonishing thing that this improvement in scoring did not take place sooner, and that influential cricketers of former days did not arrange that it should be so. (18)

It was in 1827 that wides were first recorded: no balls followed suit two years later with a run added to the total. However, although both wides and no balls were incontrovertibly perpetrated by the bowler, they did not count against him until 1985. The year of revolutions in Europe, 1848, saw a minor revolution in cricket scoring in that leg byes were first recorded as such.

The work of Britcher was taken forward by Arthur Haygarth in 1862 with the publication of Volumes 1 to 4 of *Scores and Biographies* which was his lifetime's work and recorded the scores of all known matches from 1744 to 1878. Volumes 5 to 14 were subsequently produced by MCC and published by Longman's from 1876 to 1894 and there was a final version of *Biographies* in 1925. *Wisden* came on the scene in 1864 as a modest competitor and runs alongside *Scores and Biographies* and the various *Lillywhite* publications which cover 1849 to 1900. In its very first edition, a note To the Reader expresses the hope that there might be a further edition:

Should the present work meet with but moderate success, it is intended next year to present our readers with a variety of other matches, which the confined nature of an Almanack precludes us from doing this year.

It is now in its 136th edition, universally accepted as the Cricketer's Bible and the authority on all matters of statistics and records. Like the real Bible, however, it is far from infallible and can only be as accurate as its source material. Valiant efforts continue to be made by the Association of Cricket Statisticians and Historians to minimise the errors – with no video replays of nineteenth-century matches available, it has to be accepted that they will never be eliminated entirely – but if we look at some nineteenth-century scoresheets, it is easy to see how inaccuracies can have arisen.

The slim volume that is the 1864 edition of *Wisden* makes a fascinating read. There is as full a record as was at that time possible of previous Gentlemen v Players matches with the amateurs designated either by their titles or by 'Esq' as appropriate. There are no bowling figures (as mentioned above, no bowling analysis was kept before 1840) and the subject matter extends beyond cricket to the winners of the Derby, the Oaks and the Great St Leger as it was then. There is also a note on the game of Knur and Spell, and to fill a bit of space on the last page, a few words on the trial of Charles I, some two centuries and a bit earlier!

By the mid-nineteenth century, the keeping of cricket records is well established and becoming more sophisticated. But, it is separate from official scoring, the record kept concurrently with the match, and still deals almost exclusively with batting records and statistics and the performances of batsmen. MCC in the 1890s published *Scores of Matches for the Season ... with Full Scores and Batting Averages*. The definition of 'full' does not embrace bowling figures and bowling averages are nowhere to be found; and although the recording of detailed scores of public school matches in *Wisden* declines after the Second World War, as late as the 1960s many matches are included without bowling figures. Only very slowly do bowling statistics begin to catch up.

Pratt of Sevenoaks, as we have seen was both scorer and record keeper, amateur scorer and professional printer and epitomises the bifurcation into record keeping and scoring. The historical thread of the former can be traced from Pratt through Britcher, Bentley and Haygarth to *Wisden* with its now quasi-biblical authority. It is, however, appropriate at this stage to look at the other fork, to set aside for a time the compilation of records and statistics and to look more closely at the development of scoring on paper. In accountancy terms we move back a stage from preparing the final accounts to the Books of Original Entry.

Chapter Two

Pencil and Paper

We have already seen in Chapter One that the earliest significant match of which a detailed record was kept was Kent v England XI at the Artillery Ground in 1744, but the evidence is that the record was not a concurrent one and that the notching method was in general use until beyond 1800. Throughout the second half of the eighteenth century, as cricket became more organised and codified, the two methods ran in parallel, the notchers' version providing the official record and the written unofficial version providing information for the Press.

The earliest known scoresheet which appears to have been concurrently maintained, though it may have been copied from an earlier version, is of a match between the Duke of Dorset's XI and Wrotham dated 31 August 1769. It is now in the Centre for Kentish Studies in Maidstone, (1) having come to light from among the Sackville papers only in 1959. (2)

The sheet records the first and second 'hands' of the Duke's XI. Details of the Wrotham innings were not maintained or have not survived. 'His Grace' opens the batting on both occasions and his score and those of the other members of his team are recorded in a way that has remained little changed over more than 200 years in that the value of each scoring stroke is marked alongside his name and these are then totalled to give the score for the individual innings, which in the case of John Minshull (although here he is recorded as Minchin), later of Kent and Surrey, comes to 107 to become the game's first recorded century. The sum of the individual innings along with 'by balls' gives the total for the team.

But there is no fall of wickets, no recognition of who took the wickets or the catches, certainly no bowling analysis; but an indication of the method of dismissal and in essence the rudiments of the system that has been handed on from generation to generation and can be seen in operation, weather permitting, on any school, village or club ground on any summer weekend.

In the same set of papers are the scores of three Hampshire v England matches played in 1777, at the Artillery Ground, at Guildford and at Broadhalfpenny, Hampshire. Each is for a purse of 50 guineas given respectively by Hull & Colchin, the Town of Guildford and the Gentlemen of the Hambledon Club. They differ from the 1769 sheets in that they are clearly an *ex post facto* record copied doubtless from an earlier source kept at the time of the match. The individual scores are recorded, though not the scoring strokes, but the bowlers are now credited with the wickets of batsmen they bowl and the names of the catchers are recorded, and an entry such as 'Run out Lord Tankerville's fault' is one which certainly would not be recorded by a late twentieth-century scorer unless as a lightly pencilled marginal note to assist later reports of the match. 'Thrown out by Brett', however, gives credit to the fielder in a way which is still under debate by contemporary scorers. (3)

A later scoresheet (1837) (4) recording a match between Single Men and Married Men contains the scoring shots and method of dismissal with appropriate attribution to bowler, catcher, fielder and wicket-keeper. Mr Wm. May is recorded as such whether batting or bowling; others by their surname only: perhaps we have here a forerunner of the gentleman/player distinction that was to characterise scorecards until 1962. Whether that is the case or not, he certainly plays a major role in the match, being the only man in double figures in either innings, scoring over 50 per cent of his side's runs (which notches have now become) and for good measure taking four wickets in each innings to contribute to a victory for the single men by '3 wickets and 3 runs'.

All these scoresheets, be it noted, are on plain sheets of paper. The era of the pre-printed sheet, still less of the regularly used scorebook, is not yet with us, but is not too far ahead.

The Kent Archive has a record of a match at Teddington Place on Tuesday, 31 August 1852 (5) where the innings of the Players is recorded on a pre-printed sheet with the simple headings 'Order of going in: Striker: How out: Bowler: Runs', then the same for the second innings with provision for each batsman's combined total over both innings. The score of their opponents, presumably the Gentlemen, is recorded on the back on a sheet of similar lay-out, but this time ruled by the scorer rather than pre-printed. In addition to the basics of the printed sheet, the scorer has provided for 'Fall of Wickets' and for wides, no balls and leg byes, byes being the only extras recognised by the printed version.

The lay-out was 'Entered at Stationers Hall' in accordance with the Copyright Act of 1842, an advisable though no longer compulsory registration and the accompanying advertisement informs us that 'Cricket Bats, Balls, Stumps, Chests, and Chains, with the Laws of Cricket, and New Scoring Papers are to be had of M.DARK & SONS, Bat Makers, at their Manufactory at Lord's Cricket Ground'. The advent of the scorebook was not far away.

Some might argue that it had already arrived in that the score of the first Eton v Harrow match was kept in a book rather than on a loose sheet of paper:

it is not, however, a pre-printed one, but a small quarto vellum-bound volume, containing the results of 'Upper Club' matches (Boys paid half a crown for membership) of 1805 and 1806. The book, which also records 'expenses and forfeits', was subsequently used as an accounts book, apparently by a local farmer, and between the 1805 scores at the front and the 1806 ones at the other end are a number of pages dated 1843 to 1850 which record the tithes due at Lady Day and Michaelmas, those paid, those in arrears and the amount of income tax paid.

The 1805 match was the one in which Lord Byron played and wrote in a letter preserved in the Harrow School Archives:

> We have played the Eton and were most confoundedly beat, however it was some comfort to me that I got 11 notches in the first innings and 7 the 2nd which was more than any of our side, except Brockman and Ipswich could contrive to hit ... (6)

The scorebook contradicts Byron's account which may owe something to poetic licence or it may point to the inaccuracy of the scorebook which seems to be a hybrid concurrent and *ex post facto* record, in that in the Harrow second innings the scoring strokes of the opening batsmen are recorded but not those of the other nine. It is possible that Byron's club foot caused him to bat with a runner, thereby causing confusion to the scorer – a familiar enough situation – and it may well be that this unknown Eton scorer was not particularly concerned about the accuracy of the Harrovian batting details anyway. In any event, the neutrality of the scorer was clearly not a convention he felt obliged to observe and, whatever the accuracy of his scorebook, the scorer has not restrained himself from commenting on the match by adding to the page: 'The Harrow were beat in one Innings by 12 notches easy....Hurra....Exeunt Omnes'. Modern practice would record the margin of victory as an innings and 12 runs and somewhat better arithmetic as an innings and two runs, given that the Eton innings has been erroneously totalled to 132 rather than 122. At least Lord Byron and the scorer are agreed on terminology though 'notches' are now fighting a losing battle against 'runs'.

Although this volume, purchased by Eton College in 1950 with profits from the school laundry, appears to be the earliest known scorebook, that observation needs to be qualified by the recognition that it was not a scorebook *per se* in that it was used for other purposes, was not pre-printed and, with the possible exception of the innings of the first two Harrow batsmen, was not a book of original entry, but one into which scores and results were entered from concurrently kept records.

The first known scoresheet and the first known century – Duke of Dorset's XI v Wrotham, 31 August 1769 [By permission of Lord Sackville and the Centre for Kentish Studies]

It does, however, precede by more than 20 years what Robert Brooke and Peter Matthews claim to be the oldest cricket scorebook, that for the Oxford v Cambridge fixture in 1829.(7) It is not pre-printed, the method of scoring is the same as that used in the Eton v Harrow match and there seems no good reason to call it a first. Obviously, Brooke and Matthews were unaware of the little vellum-bound volume residing in the library of Eton College.

There are references to earlier scorebooks, though the likelihood is that these were of the Britcher type and historical rather than contemporary records of matches. In his *Annals of Lord's and History of the* MCC Alfred D. Taylor refers to the original scorebook of the old Homerton Club which covered a period from 1802 to 1808 and was maintained by Benjamin Aislabie who later became the first Secretary of the MCC. (8) Likewise, in the Preface to the first volume of *Scores and Biographies*, Haygarth refers to his sources as 'scores, old score books, newspapers etc' and mentions later that 'often in the old score books the order of the sides going in is reversed'. (9)

The 'Upper Club' books at Eton re-emerge in 1834 when some matches are scored 'live' in pencil and are then inked in. They then continue in an unbroken sequence beyond the end of the century and it is these, rather than the original scorebooks which are clearly intended to be the official record of the club. In 1859, for instance, the Captain, the Hon. C.G. Lyttelton, a member of a distinguished cricketing family, who succeeded as the 8th Viscount Cobham in 1888, records:

> The scores of one or two games played in Collection Week cannot be recorded owing to the loss of the scoring-book, a piece of carelessness by no means attributable to the Captain.

Notwithstanding the fact that these are not books of original entry, they are of interest for the way in which they illustrate developments in the recording of the game and the light they throw on cricket language and terminology. For instance, a lead is described as 'above tye', a defeat by 10 wickets (or perhaps more, where matches are more than eleven-a-side) is recorded as 'beat by every wicket'; at first, Byes are the only extras recorded and 'hit his wicket' as a method of dismissal is a not-infrequent entry.

In some ways, the books are more informative than contemporary ones recording first-class cricket: certainly, being the product of two annually appointed keepers (the captain and one other) they are more literate, reflecting a different standard of education, and throwing light on the role of the Upper Club, an autonomous body within the College, and one whose activities are not always sanctioned by the authorities. The match between the Eton Eleven and University College Oxford on 11 June 1859 ended on the following sad note:

> This match was unfortunately unfinished as no leave was given to the Eleven by the Headmaster. University therefore won by 72 runs.

Matches not played out were determined on the first innings.

Among the first purpose-printed scorebooks were those published in 1851 and 'entered at Stationers' Hall' in 1852 by Thomas Mellard of Stousbridge [sic], the 'Roby's All England Eleven Cricket Match Scoring Book' and the 'All England Cricket Match Scoring Book'. Slightly earlier in the same register is an entry for 'Lillywhite and Sons Registered Cricket Scoring Paper'. (10) The inference must be therefore that it is around this time that the score*sheet* yields to the score*book*.

That the printed scoresheet was well established by this time is clear from Rev. James Pycroft's contemporary *The Cricket Field* where old and new methods are compared:

> What wonder that notches on a stick, like the notches on the milk-woman's tally in Hogarth's picture, should supply the place of those complicated papers of vertical columns, which subject the bowling, the batting and the fielding to a

Match played at   Oval   on Sep 6th

First Innings.

Order of going in	Names of the Batsmen	Runs as scored	How Out	Name of Bowler
1	E M Grace Esq	141141411211121412) 1141412	c Alexander	Bannerman
2	W G Grace Esq	3341211141311311211311 412221111 41111231134111433222111211121 4111241	Bowled	Palmer
3	A P Lucas Esq	121131441241212111124211124	Bowled	Bannerman
4	Barnes	421133213313)	Bowled	Alexander
5	Lord Harris	21116141124122611141211161	c Bonner	Alexander
6	F. Penn Esq	312112144)	Bowled	Bannerman
7	A G Steel	141111321441322341 41	c Boyle	Moule
8	Hon A Lyttleton	41231	not out	
9	G F Grace	0	c Bannerman	Moule
10	Shaw	0	Bowled	Moule
11	Morley	2	Run out	
	Byes	1124		
	Leg Byes	1311211		
	Wide Balls			
	No Balls			
				Total of First Innings

Runs at the fall of each Wicket: 1 for 91 2 for 211 3 for 269 4 for 281 5 for 322 6 for 404 7 for 410 8 for 410 9 for 413 10 for

Second Innings

Order of going in		Runs as scored	How Out	Name of Bowler
1	Hon Lyttleton	114111Q	Bowled	Palmer
2	G F Grace		Bowled	Palmer
3	A P Lucas	11	c Blackham	Palmer
4	F Penn	131111242 4124	not out	
5	Barnes	41	c Moule	Boyle
6	E M Grace		Bowled	Boyle
7	W G Grace	11141		
8				
9				
10				
11				
	Byes			
	Leg Byes			
	Wide Balls	1		
	No Balls	1		
				Total of Second Innings
				Total of Both Innings

Runs at the fall of each Wicket: 1 for 2 2 for 10 3 for 22 4 for 31 5 for 31 6 for 7 for 8 for 9 for 10 for

Scoresheet of the first Test Match played in England: England v Australia at The Oval

YSIS OF BOWLING, SHOWING NUMBER OF BALLS BOWLED & RUNS MADE FROM EACH BOWLER.

First Innings.

of Bowler	1	2	3	4	5	6	7	8	9	10	11	12	13	14	15	16	17	18	19	20	Wide Balls	No Balls

SUMMARY OF BOWLING.

of Bowler.	Total N° of Balls	N° of maiden overs	Total N° of runs	N° of Wickets	N° of wide Balls	N° of no Balls
e	41	15	71	0		
mr	40	27	116	1		
ander	32	10	69	2		
nirman	50	12	111	3		
nall	9	0	11	0		
le	12	4	23	3		

SUMMARY OF BOWLING. (Continued)

Name of Bowler.	Total N° of Balls	N° of maiden overs	Total N° of Runs	N° of Wickets	N° of wide Balls	N° of no Balls

YSIS OF BOWLING, SHOWING NUMBER OF BALLS BOWLED & RUNS MADE FROM EACH BOWLER.

Second Innings.

e of Bowler	1	2	3	4	5	6	7	8	9	10	11	12	13	14	15	16	17	18	19	20	Wide Balls	No Balls

SUMMARY OF BOWLING.

of Bowler	Total N° of Balls	N° of maiden overs	Total N° of Runs	N° of Wickets	N° of wide Balls	N° of no Balls
yle	17	7	21	2		
mr	16	5	35	3		1

SUMMARY OF BOWLING. (Continued)

Name of Bowler	Total N° of Balls	N° of maiden overs	Total N° of Runs	N° of Wickets	N° of wide Balls	N° of no Balls

6, 7 & 8 September 1880 [Reproduced by kind permission of Surrey County Cricket Club] process severely and scrupulously just, of analytical observation or differential calculus. (11)

Other evidence – at least as far as 'official' scoring is concerned – is that the analysis to which the bowling and fielding were subjected at this time was negligible. Despite the mid-nineteenth-century hyperbole, the point that cricket scoring is beginning to be more complicated is well made and, as we shall see in the next chapter, the Press were beginning to be more innovative.

Until this point, source material for this study of the history of scoring has been sparse and spasmodic. But we now reach the point of Victorian expansionism when the railways facilitate travelling, when professional XIs begin to emerge, when the public schools, having imported the game through the sons of the aristocracy, impose on it the image of muscular Christianity, when county clubs and others are established. In short, the game expands, scorebooks proliferate and the methodology of research changes from seeking out the few to selecting from the many.

As far as county scorebooks are concerned, I have based my investigations mainly on those of Surrey and Hampshire, largely because of geographical convenience, but the evidence is that the evolution of scoring in these two counties has not been markedly different from what has transpired elsewhere. (12)

It might be possible to draw a more logical and consistent picture from the records of a single county, but recent research by the Association of Cricket Statisticians and Historians has discovered that only two of the first-class counties (Yorkshire and Durham) have a complete run of scorebooks. (13) All the others have gaps. Surrey have huge ones, books for only three seasons between 1886 and 1958 having survived. Ironically, this 73 year period was covered almost entirely by two of scoring's most distinguished servants, Fred Boyington from 1884 to 1926 and Herbert Strudwick from 1928 to 1957. Both were responsible for the copyrighting of scoresheet design, yet next to nothing survives of the work of either of them – or if more survive, then their whereabouts are unknown to the Club.

The scorebooks that were used in first-class matches in the nineteenth century were large ledger-type volumes with sheets of foolscap or larger size that owe much to the theory and practice of double-entry book-keeping, runs being credited to the batsman, debited to the bowler and balanced at the end of the innings. Indeed, those used by Somerset towards the end of the century, supplied by F.S. & A. Robinson and Co., Account Book Manufacturers, Bristol, and now housed in the County Club's museum, are ruled into various lines, columns and squares, but contain no headings and leave to the scorer an element of discretion in the entering of information.

Surrey's early scorebooks are not particularly well maintained. A number contain loose pages which do not always relate to the year of the book concerned and in many cases, neither the date of the match, nor the participating teams are identified. Sometimes, it has been possible to remedy these deficiencies by the use of other sources, but the scorebook as a primary source of historical and statistical information was a foreign concept to the Club and its scorers in the mid-nineteenth century.

The earliest book is that for 1856 and the record is kept – albeit incompletely on occasions – on 'Frederick Lillywhite's Registered Scoring Sheet' which advertises in the bottom right-hand corner 'All articles concerned with cricket supplied'. Provision for the entry of the batting details of both innings is on the left-hand page under the headings Order of Going In, Name of the Batsman, Figures as Scored, How Out, Bowler's Name, Runs. Below the batsmen's names, there are spaces to enter Byes, Leg Byes, Wide Balls, No Balls and Runs at the Fall of Each Wicket. Then we have Total of First Innings, Total of Second Innings, Total of the Two Innings. Apart from the mid-nineteenth-century verbosity and two innings on the same page, it all looks pretty familiar.

'The Analysis of the Bowling' on the opposite page looks somewhat less familiar. The headings here are Bowler's Name, No Balls, Wide Balls, The Number of Overs and The Runs made from Bowlers etc., then, summarised below, Total no of No Balls, Total no of Wide Balls, Total no of Balls, Total no of Runs, Total no of Maiden Overs, Total no of Wickets, then Notes and the whole thing is repeated for the second innings. Rarely are the details completed entirely, often they are not completed at all, a reflection of their perceived importance at the time.

Some of the entries are copied in from other records; the first match (v Oxfordshire on 3 and 4 June) contains no bowling analysis and in the second (v Sussex on 20 and 21 June), the Fall of Wickets is incomplete, but the book does reflect both the cricketing and social climate of the time and contains some famous names. The amateurs are designated by 'Esqre', Wisden and James Lillywhite are in the Sussex side, overs in minor matches, such as that against Islington Albion Club on 23 July, are of six rather than four balls, the size of the Kennington Oval's playing area is reflected in several 5s and the occasional 7, different handwriting suggests the absence of a regular scorer and standards of scoring and literacy are indicated by numerous deletions and 'J Ceasar b Wisdon 0', though in the capital in July, rather than on the Capitol in March.

These early scorers, however, were not averse to including the odd comment or opinion in the scorebook. On 8 September 1857 in the Surrey v Manchester with two players match, we find Surrey's no 11 Martingell '(so said) Leg B W b Wisden 0' and later in 1863, in the Surrey v North of England fixture at Broughton, E. Stephenson, for the North, having been run out 0 in the first innings, is recorded in the second as 'absent – shamefully and disgracefully 0'.

Inserted in the book which covers the 1856–58 seasons is a loose sheet, printed in 1857, which is 'not intended to Score upon (though it has been!) but for the purpose of copying the result' and submitting it to *Bell's Life in London*. Significantly, there is no provision on the sheet for bowling figures, but equally significantly they are on their way. The scorebook used in 1862–63 has been subject to some streamlining: for instance, in the headings 'Total no of...' has been reduced to 'Total...' and on the title page, there is the instruction from *Bell's Life*: 'To find out your best bowlers, it is requisite that you should analyze the bowling yearly, and average from it each over...'

Printed at the back of the book are 'Explanations': Lillywhite obviously takes the view by this stage that scorers are in need of some instruction and provides it in some detail. It precedes the training courses of the Association of Cricket Umpires and Scorers by a century or so and it is illuminating to quote it in full:

> For the information of those who are inexperienced in 'Cricket Match Scoring' or the game itself (both being two very difficult tasks to accomplish) the following illustration is given, whereby a person who may know a little of the game can sufficiently fulfil the situation:
>
> FIRST LINE After the word 'at', the name of the place you are playing at. After the word 'between' put the name of each side. After 'on' put the date.
>
> SECOND LINE Before the words 'first innings', the name of the party who first takes the wicket.
>
> The FIRST COLUMN will show the order of going in.
>
> The SECOND COLUMN the names of the batsmen as they go to their wickets.
>
> THIRD COLUMN Place a figure down for the number of runs the batsman gets each hit, the double line being ruled for a long score.
>
> The FOURTH COLUMN will show how the player was out.
>
> The FIFTH COLUMN who bowled the ball, viz if he is stumped or caught put down 'st' for stumped and 'c' for caught , by whoever did it, under the head

'how out', and the bowler's name in the fifth column.

It has been suggested by the author of this work, through the medium of 'Bell's Life', that the following alteration should take place – When a man is 'run out' place under the head 'how out' 'run out' by whoever may have put the wicket down and thrown by whoever threw the ball. For instance, if Box puts the wicket down from Parr it should be placed thus:

'run out' Box 't' Parr.

The SIXTH COLUMN shows the total number of runs the player obtained in his first innings.

'Leg byes' and 'Byes' to be kept separate.

'Wides' and 'No Balls' to be scored to the bowler who bowls them, as well as their proper place. 'Runs at the fall of every wicket' can be easily kept by adding the score up when the player is out and placing it after the printed figure of the number of wickets down.

BOWLERS' OVERS &c

FIRST COLUMN – If he should bowl a 'No Ball'
SECOND COLUMN – If he should bowl a wide
THIRD COLUMN – The bowler's name.

The remaining small columns are for the 'bowler's overs' and the 'runs' obtained from them. If the batsman makes a hit for one and then three place that number to the bowler who bowled the ball after you have placed it to the batsman's name. When a ball is bowled and no run obtained place a 'dot' immediately the ball is bowled (for instance, 13...); by so doing you will be able to analyze the bowling after the match is over. For that purpose lines have been ruled at the side where you may place the 'total number of balls bowled' by each bowler, 'number of runs' got from his bowling, the number of 'maiden overs' he bowled, and his number of wickets; and at the end of the season the bowling can be analyzed, so as to procure the information required.

There is then a reference to *Lillywhite's Guide to Cricketers* for the 'Celebrated Bowlers in England'. All fairly elementary stuff and something of an idiot's guide, but as lucid an exposition of the principles of scoring as was available at the time. The concept of bowlers as fifth columnists is an

The 'Strudwick' scoresheet as currently used by decreasing numbers of county scorers. [By kind permission of Surrey County Cricket Club]

interesting anachronism, the recommended attribution of run outs was not acted upon at the time and even now is a custom more honoured in the breach than the observance.

By 1862 it appears as though Surrey had a regular scorer or at least someone, possibly the Secretary, who was making regular entries in a book, for the handwriting is now more consistent, but it is clear that some matches are copied from earlier versions, the bowling analysis is not always included and when it is, it is frequently incomplete. The regular appearance of audit-type ticks confirms the impression that the figures are being checked against others and that this is not concurrent scoring. Indeed, in the Surrey v North of England match at Broughton, Manchester on 14 August there is a pencilled marginal note to the effect that 'Caffyns [sic] innings should be 18'. Maybe it should but the smudged entry in the book of 113411131 totals to 16!

In 1863 most of the scoring is live and concurrent and a couple of the matches – against Sussex at Brighton on 13 July and Yorkshire at Bramall Lane, Sheffield on 27 July – although entered in barely legible pencilled scrawl, contain a deal more information than is generally available in contemporary scoresheets. For instance, bowling spells are recorded – unusual at the time – and there are small annotations over some of the scoring shots e.g. c, sql, e, d (cover, square leg, edge, drive (or draw?)) The score at

BOWLER	BOWLING ANALYSIS										Overs	Maidens	Runs	Wickets	Wides	No Balls
	1	2	3	4	5	6	7	8	9	10						
..M											3	-	15	4		
..J											4	-	13	.	1	
..LL											13·1	6	27	4	2	
..CK											12	2	42	5		
MINS / OVER		50 / 67 / 14·4	100 / 148 / 31·3													
TOTAL											32·1	8	104	10	1	2

This one shows Australia's second innings in the Final Test of the 1997 series

close of play is recorded and there are notes on where the batsman was caught and sometimes on the quality of the dismissal e.g. skyer, long-mid-off, mid wkt, good catch. There is marginal arithmetic, the score at the end of each over and a cryptic marginal note which reads '£2 £3 v Yorks Barber', though whether this is a note on a wager, a fee or a very expensive haircut will remain for ever a mystery. There is the odd reference to the timing of an innings and to targets, for example, 'Yorks 1st inns finished half-3' or '20 to 2 Wednesday to get 174 to win' and, finally, in the Sussex match, 'Result of match – Drawn match in favour of Surrey half-past 5 o'c'. I wonder whether the Sussex version records the result in the same way.

And so it goes on. Not only Surrey's matches are recorded, but other matches played at the Kennington Oval e.g. Gents of North v Gents of South, Married of England v Single of England, Players of England v Australia. Some of the matches are scored in an elegant copperplate hand, others in a barely legible scrawl; some record the bare minimum of information, others have excited marginal notes – Monday Night No wicket for 100 runs! or a triple exclamation mark for Jas Lillywhite's bowling figures of 101-38-154-6. They were admittedly four-ball overs, but it still represents quite a spell.

There is useful material for both social and cricket historian in these pages and certainly some interesting stories behind the scoresheets. In September

1871, Surry [sic] play 22 Colts of Surrey. The Colts make 116 (for 21) in their first innings: Southerton takes 12 for 51; they do slightly better in their second innings, registering 189 for 17 – Southerton 7-32. The next time the equivalent fixture is played, it becomes 21 colts with Southerton v 11 of the County, though Southerton in one of several juvenile hands is written with his S and N in reverse script and two of the Colts with the same name are distinguished as 'Jones Carshalton' and 'Jones Mitcham'.

Edward J. Page buys out the late F. Lillywhite and the registered score sheet and privilege of publishing the same and they can now be procured only from the said E.J. Page. There are other scoresheets around, however. J. Wisden and Co. and Arrowsmith of Bristol are publishing a sheet where the batting and bowling of one innings are on the same page and a match against Nottinghamshire in the 1870s is recorded on a scoresheet printed and published by Richard Daft (member of the All England XI) at his Cricket and British Sports Warehouse and presumably purloined for the occasion from the opposition's scorebook. This has provision for the order of going in and the order of coming out and there are also spaces for a 'Grand Summary' of bowling figures. It has not, however, been completed.

Although I have headed this chapter, Pencil and Paper, some have been completed in ink, some in blue crayon and some in a mixture of two of the three. At some matches, there is evidence of more than one scorer or the official scorer arriving late, there are a number of arithmetical errors and although these documents are and must be primary sources for cricket historians and statisticians, there are instances where it must be questionable whether they accurately reflect what went on in the match.

At times, the loose bits of paper that have found their way into the books are perhaps of more interest than the scores themselves – the more important of which have found their way to secondary sources anyway. There is a curt note to the scorers in the 1876 book, presumably from a club official – 'Scorers put up the full total at Lunch Time' – presumably a reference to the fact that on the old 'Telegraphs' the total was put up only in tens.

Then, there is a loose press cutting which refers to W.G. Grace's 400 not out for the United South of England against Twenty-two of the Worsley Club at Grimsby in 1876 which noted that 'some who witnessed the game go so far as to assert that had all the runs he made been correctly entered his total should have exceeded that of Mr Tylecote'. E.F.S. Tylecote had scored 404 not out for the Classical against the Modern side at Clifton College, a record in any kind of cricket at the time. So there we have it: a probable world record, but no public confidence in the competence of the scorers of the time!

The only Test Match in the collection in the County Record Office (14) is that of 1884 which saw the first double century in Test cricket (W.L.

Murdoch's 211) and was the only occasion in Test cricket when 11 bowlers were used in one innings. The book containing the Test which gave birth to The Ashes in 1882 is on the AWOL list, but the jewel in the crown, the scorebook containing the 1880 Test is kept in the Library at what is now The Foster's Oval – and it's wrong!

The number of overs and maidens bowled by Boyle in England's first innings have been incorrectly totalled to 41 and 15 respectively (and the maidens have clearly been amended from an earlier and even more incorrect 14). An examination of the scoresheet, however, reveals that part of the third line of the analysis has been disregarded and that on that line are two more maiden overs.

Wisden for the following year takes its statistics from the scoresheet and gives the figures as 41-15-71-0. Bill Frindall, whose statistics correct a number of earlier official versions (15) (including Arthur Wrigley's which is as recent as 1965), as a result of research of the original scorebooks, improves the record to 44-17-71-0, but the earlier incorrect 41-15-71-0 was part of the official record for more than 80 years. It is difficult therefore to avoid the cynical conclusion that, notwithstanding the detailed and meticulous work of the Association of Cricket Statisticians and Historians (see Chapter Eleven) some Test cricket records have been wrong from the time of the very first Test match played in England!

There are other examples of the official version differing from what actually took place on the field of play. But it is only recently that cricket scoring has been regarded as anything of a profession and even the most presumptuous and immodest of current scorers would not claim infallibility. Some of the early records were kept by well-intentioned amateurs and although inaccuracies have subsequently been reduced, they can never be entirely eliminated.

Scores and statistics reflect in general terms what has happened on the field of play, but the spurious accuracy of batting and bowling averages, scoring rates and over rates calculated to two or three places of decimals, can only give rise to a healthy cynicism and pleas to desist from paralysis by analysis where what is being analysed is more than slightly suspect.

By the end of the nineteenth century, the scorebook was virtually ubiquitous at both County and Club level and advertisements by a number of manufacturers – West, Bourne, Dean and Hayes among others – began to appear regularly in *Wisden* and other cricket publications. There was now a greater interest in the art of scoring and a recognition of the need to recruit and train scorers. Charles Box, in his authoritative work *The English Game of Cricket*, published in 1877, (16) has, after the Laws of Cricket, a short section on 'The Theory of Scoring' in which he has this to say:

ANALYSIS OF THE BOWLING—FIRST INNINGS.

BOWLERS.	No Balls.	Wide Balls.	No. of "OVERS" AND RUNS MADE FROM EACH B
			1 2 3 4 5 6 7 8 9
C. M. SHARPE			....｜....｜..3.｜....｜....｜ 3...｜....｜.3.｜.4.2｜.1..｜....｜12..｜....
			...1｜....｜ 4...｜...1｜...3｜....｜.1.｜1...｜..3.｜....｜....｜....｜....
			...4｜ 4...｜..w.1｜.1.w｜.1.1｜...1｜..2.｜....｜4..2｜...3｜...3｜...1.｜....
			...4｜....｜ 2...｜....｜....｜....｜....｜....｜1...｜....｜..1｜.1.w｜....｜1...
			...1｜....｜ 2...｜...2｜....｜..2.｜....｜ 3.2.｜....｜1..2｜...1｜....｜1...
			....｜..1.｜.w..｜..w｜	
H. M. SIMS	1		..3.｜..3.｜1...｜1...｜...1｜....｜11..｜....｜....｜...1｜....｜..21｜.2..
	1		..1｜1..2｜11..｜...1｜....｜.1.2｜1...｜....｜..w.｜....｜....｜..w.｜.2..
W. S. PATTERSON			....｜...1｜....｜....｜ 4...｜..11｜....｜....｜....｜....｜....｜....｜....
			2...｜ 4...｜..4.｜.2..｜....｜ 1...｜....｜....｜..w.｜..32｜....｜...1｜....
			w...｜ 3...｜1...｜.2..｜....｜ 2.1.｜....｜..1｜4.1.｜....｜2...｜..2w｜....
			..1.｜.212｜	
F. J. GREENFIELD			.4..｜....｜..13｜.1..｜....｜....｜ 1...｜	

BOWLERS' NAMES.	Total No Balls.	Total Wide Balls.	Total Balls.	Total Maidens, Overs.	Total Runs.	Total Wickets.	BOWLERS' NAMES—con.	Total No Balls.	Total Wide Balls.	Total Balls.	Total Maidens, Overs.	Total Runs.	Total Wickets.
1. C. M. SHARPE			274	29	89	5	6.						
2. H. M. SIMS		2	104	10	30	2	7.						
3. W. S. PATTERSON			164	21	51	3	8.						
4. F. J. GREENFIELD			28	3	10		9.						
5.							10.						

Charles Box's example of how the bowling analysis should be completed (1877)

In scanning these pages, or even a portion of them, the eye of the reader must have been frequently arrested by the word 'score', and probably strange ideas of the mode by which it is compounded have been entertained. A few words on this subject may, therefore, be quite fitting here. Seeing that it is not easy always to obtain a person quite *au fait* in the art of scoring, the aid of the nonprofessional becomes an absolute necessity. This duty is often avoided, either in the ground of diffidence or expressed incapacity. Now if the former cannot be easily cured the latter can. Provided with a proper score sheet, the rudimentary principles can be mastered in a single lesson; thus, if a batsman makes a hit for a single, mark the figure one against his name: if three, add that figure thereto, and so on till he completes his innings; next, add all those figures together, and place them against his name in the total column. The same process must be adopted with every batsman until the innings is completed. On every well constructed score sheet there is a line denoting the number of runs totalled at the fall of each wicket, thus:

1	2	3	4	5	6	7	8	9	10
86	90	133	140	147	150	186	193	195	200

What can be easier? The analysis of bowling seems at first sight a difficult operation, but it is more apparent than real. Care and attention are the chief requisites, yet some knowledge of the game is desirable.

There then follows reference to the scoresheet of the 1875 Varsity Match, which is reproduced from the MCC book, and the passage continues:

> Members of the sporting press enter more minutely into it, by describing the changes of bowling and the precise point at which a wide or no-ball enters into the calculation; but the fore going may be regarded as being sufficient for general purposes ...

A somewhat more concise set of instructions than Lillywhite's earlier tutorial and an admission that the Press kept a more detailed and possibly more accurate score than the official scorers. No mention of checking the score, no mention of scorers co-operating and no mention of balancing batting and bowling statistics – but at least we have the rudiments of a *vade mecum* of traditional scoring which has survived largely unchanged, albeit with some later refinements, until the present day.

With the new century came further developments in the now well-established art of cricket scoring, but we have also reached the point where there is a large gap in Surrey's records and we shall need to turn elsewhere for examples of these developments.

Chapter Three

Linear Scoring and the Contemporary Scene

As the twentieth century unfolds differently from the nineteenth, so do its scorebooks as the Victorian ledgers are gradually abandoned and replaced by books, which, although they continue to use the same double entry debit and credit system, are now of more manageable size and shape, coming in landscape rather than portrait format. We have now reached the period where there is a void of over 50 years in the sequence of Surrey's scorebooks and so turn our attention to Hampshire (1) who first contested the County Championship in 1895.

The book in use at this time is similar to those used by Surrey, but is John Wisden & Co.'s *Cricketers' Scoring Book (Greatly Improved)* 'containing the batsman's score and an analysis of the bowling' and, according to the frontispiece publicity with the same naive optimism that assumed the sun would never set on the British Empire, 'arranged so simply that a novice cannot make any mistakes in keeping a correct score'.

The book provided for 50 matches and cost twelve shillings and sixpence, but also advertised are those containing 100 matches for £1, 25 for 7s 6d or scoring sheets at 2s 6d per dozen.

The entries contain nothing unusual or exceptional in that, like many of the entries in the Surrey books considered earlier, they are fair copies based on earlier concurrent records and the bowling analysis of Cambridge University is not deemed worthy of recording.

In the 1920s there is a change of book to *The 'Ideal' British Cricket Score Book* 'revised and re-arranged by F Boyington, Official Scorer, Surrey County Cricket Club'. It is also used by Somerset and probably by a number of other counties. The nature of the information recorded is little different, although there is now provision for 'Side winning toss for choice of Innings' and we have a double-page spread for one innings with the batting on the left-hand page and the bowling on the right.

The design is essentially the same as that of current-day scorebooks, except that those used in club cricket – the 'Bourne' and 'Thomas' probably being the best known – usually have an 'accumulator' where the runs are crossed off a pre-printed chart as scored and additionally the bowling analysis is printed below rather than alongside the batting with a box inclining to a square rather than an elongated rectangle, so that the individual balls of an over are recorded on two lines or columns of three rather than one line of six.

For one season, 1927, Hampshire introduced the 'Somerset' book, nothing to do with the eponymous county, but the brainchild of one A.F. Somerset who put it on the market in 1912. It is an attempt to embellish traditional scoring by the introduction of more detail, but as far as Hampshire is concerned it was a spectacular failure and the county reverted to the Boyington book for the 1928 season. It is worth while looking at what Somerset was trying to do, however, as some of his ideas are a few years in advance of their time and in later years came to be regarded if not as part of the official record, then certainly as part of the optional extras which enable a game to be replayed in the mind from a well-kept scorebook.

This book is an attempt to increase the interest in the game by giving something more than is the custom in the score-books generally used. In apologizing to the scorers, I hope that the extra trouble involved will be compensated by the thought that the course of the game will be made more comprehensible for others to follow after it is over. Two inches are provided for each name and half-an-inch square for each over of the bowler's analysis. A space is left for remarks on each innings, for umpires' and scorers' names, for the duration of each batsman's innings, and for that of the innings as a whole; also for the state of the wicket, the weather, and the wind - which three latter have an important bearing on the score made, and can usually be summed up in a word or two by a cricketer. There is also space for the record of interruptions caused by rain, light etc, and one for palpable catches dropped. I hope the scorers will not be too hard on the fielders in this particular, remembering that some fielders will get to a catch and make it look like a chance, which others would not get near; also the snick which is heard all over the ground is an impossible catch for the wicket-keeper standing up, for the ball is turned too much. Still, dropped catches have such an important bearing on the score that I think palpable ones should be recorded ...

He then goes on to advise:

Put a broad line thus: – | when a bowler is taken off... 'c' over the batsman's

A MATCH on *Wednesday* **the** *11* **of**

Between _Between eleven of the Burwoo..._

Burwood   1ST INNINGS.

Order of going in.	Striker.	How out.	Bowler.	Mudie	Street	Runs got from
1	J. Payne	Bowled	Street	41221	13	
2	J. Faulkner	caught down	Street			
3	W. Beard	C: Mudie	Street	11	1	
4	Mr F Sheppington	C: Harrison	Street	241	1112	
5	J. Pratt	Bowled	Mudie		1	
6	F Spyers	C: Street C: Paisley	Street	1		
7	J. Thorpe	C: Paisley	Street			
8	Martineau Esq	C: Harrison	Mudie	1		
9	H. Spyers	C: Beard	Street	1		
10	F Burnett	Not Out		1	4	
11	F Meyer Esq	Bowled	Mudie			
		Byes		1	212	
		Leg Byes		1		
		Wide Balls				
		No Balls				

Printed and Sold by J. D. Mills, 9, Lavender Villas, Wandsworth Road;

An early example of rudimentary linear scoring – Burwood v Surrey Club and Ground at Hersh

185*8*, at _Heckham_

and eleven of the Surrey Club and ground

2ND INNINGS.

How out.	Bowler.	Runs got from Mudie	Hunt	Dawson	Total 2nd Inn.	Grand Total.
c Mudie	Street	31	22		8	22
c Payne	Street	1	2		3	3
~~Bowled~~	Street	234	214	4141	27	30
c Dawson	Mudie				0	12
not out			21112	1111	13	14
Bowled	Street			223	7	8
Bowled	Street				0	0
Bowled	Street				0	1
Run out				22	4	6
run out				1	1	6
c Page	Dawson				0	0
		2.	1	1	4	10
			11		2	8
				1	1	1
					70	115

Mills's Pocket Edition of the " Laws of Cricket," price 6d., in a case 1s.

11 August 1858 [Reproduced by kind permission of Surrey County Cricket Club]

score for every palpable catch dropped and in the bowlers analysis.

Some scorers still use the 'c' method for recording missed chances. Clem Driver of Essex has a further refinement. A missed half-chance is recorded as 'c/2'. Back to Somerset, however:

> I welcome corrections and a blank space is provided for records and curiosities which may happen, and which I shall always be glad to have a note of ...

He then digresses from scoring *per se* into an interesting historical footnote:

> The game has now taken so firm a hold that it has probably become the greatest common interest of the British Empire. The Dutch in South Africa have learnt to love it, and who can tell how great an influence the game may have on cementing the union of the white races ...

Since then, apartheid has been and gone, South Africa has been in and out of Test cricket and the 'Dutch' have stuffed England out of sight 6-1 in a One Day series.

Rarely were Somerset's scoresheets completed in full, though the times of the beginning and end of batsmen's innings usually were and the state of the wicket at The Oval when Hampshire play Surrey is described as 'plumb easy'. Little change there. The names of umpires and scorers were usually entered and it is of passing interest to note that the Surrey scorer in this match in the season between Boyington's death and Strudwick's appointment was Alfred Pilkington who played his sole first-class match the previous season, did a bit of scoring in 1927, then disappeared from the scene.

By 1930 the 'Boyington' scorebook had become the 'Cambridge', and, although almost identical in layout, has a couple of refinements. There is provision for the time in and time out of the batsmen and for the number of the outgoing batsman at the fall of each wicket. A book of similar design is used by Cambridge University today. In an article in 1930, two years into his 30-year career as Surrey's scorer, Herbert Strudwick refers to the range of books in use on the county circuit, noting that MCC and one or two other counties use Wisden's book, some counties use the Somerset book and that Kent and Yorkshire have their own set of books. (2)

The transition to the Strudwick scorebook occurred in the late 1930s and it is this design, with no modifications of any significance, printed by Telen Printing of Whitstable, that has been used by most county clubs until the 1990s when it is superseded by the computer and found wanting as a back-up manual record. There is plenty of space for a huge innings by any batsman and for some 340 overs by up to nine bowlers. There is now provision for noting the time (though not the balls) taken for a batsman to reach 50, 100, 150 and 200, for the batsman out and batsman not out at the fall of a wicket and a few lines for remarks which scorers have generally used for noting interval scores and the innings time taken for 50, 100 etc. But nowhere is there provision for the score at the end of each over, for the number of balls received by each batsman, times of partnerships etc. Consequently, as more information is required by the media, most scorers have found it necessary either to keep supplementary sheets or develop individual systems based on the linear principle – of which more later.

Michael Fordham and Eddie Solomon demonstrate how the conventional system can be used to calculate balls faced without resorting to a full linear system:

> A simpler form of [the linear method] using a conventional score book is to record the balls received by each batsman on a separate sheet of paper at the end of each over. The easiest way to achieve this is to divide the bowlers analysis into upper and lower areas recording balls faced by each batsman in turn. (3)

It is possible to record balls faced in the batting section of the scoresheet and a number of club scorers tend to use this method. It is not particularly satisfactory, however, when information on the number of balls faced is required immediately rather than at the end of the innings.

Other variations on the conventional scoresheet try to cram in as much information as possible into a small space. That produced by the Australian Cricket Board and in use in first-class cricket throughout Australia allows for interval scores, the time of bowling changes, the length of partnerships, the time in minutes and overs for each 50, the number of balls in each partnership and the number of runs and overs in each hour.

The sheet used by the United Cricket Board of South Africa has all of that and goes the extra mile in providing space for the total at the end of each half-hour and the time and overs for each ten runs. Additonally, the squares for the bowling analysis are sub divided into four mini-columns, though whether this is a relic from the days of eight-ball overs or the additional space assumes an average of a wide and a no ball per over is not evident.

The Women's Cricket Association, in addition to the conventional scoresheet which recorded the usual information, had at the 1993 World Cup a supplementary A3 sheet comprising a matrix of thirty-three columns, three for each batsman, and sixty lines, one for each over. At the end of each over, Time, Balls and Runs for the batsmen at the crease are recorded and additionally, the balls and runs in each partnership, as well as the details of the batsmen out and not out.

Commendable though this attention to detail may be, the system suffers two main disadvantages; firstly, two scorers are required to operate it, one to complete the conventional scoresheet and the other to complete the information required at the end of each over (the over rate in women's cricket is so much higher than in men's and consequently three or four balls have gone in the next over before the details of the previous one are fully recorded); and secondly, it is usually the case that at any one time 27 of the 33 columns are unused.

However, the method does attempt to address the convention of recording balls faced in a tidier way than entering them in the batting section on the scoresheet where there can be space problems and where it is, if not impossible to reconcile who bowled what to whom, then certainly cumbersome and tortuous. It is, nevertheless, the method recommended in the latest edition of what is generally considered to be the standard text book on scoring; (4) but current opinion is that the challenge of providing more detail and analysing the progress of play is met by the practice of linear scoring, to which we now turn.

Generally considered to have been the invention of W.H. Ferguson, the legendary 'Fergie' on the 1905 Australian tour of England, (5) linear scoring is based on the matrix principle of having one line per over, one column for each batsman and recording changes to the principal statistics at the end of each over. Thus it is much easier to analyse than with the conventional system who did what and with what and to whom and at what time.

As early as 1858, J.D. Mills was printing a scoresheet which had the rudiments of linear scoring with a fairly crude matrix, was capable of analysing from which bowlers the batsmen had scored their runs with the 'Runs as scored' section replaced by 'Runs got from' and a column for each bowler. Thus, the principle of one entry per ball from which both batting and bowling statistics may be calculated emerges, though unlike later and more sophisticated versions of linear scoring, it is not possible to trace the course of the innings.

In his autobiography, Ferguson tells the story of how he began a 50-year career as scorer and baggage master by visiting Monty Noble's dental surgery and talking himself on to the 1905 tour. (6) He had no previous scoring experience, but soon found the traditional method inadequate and, using a school exercise book, designed a method of scoring that has one line per over and one entry per ball and allows the progress of the game to be followed ball-by-ball far more easily than the traditional method. Pycroft's reference in Chapter Two to 'those complicated papers of vertical columns' would seem to imply the existence of linear scoring and there is evidence however that the Press (and we have already noted in Chapter One that 'unofficial' scoring by the media tends to be in advance in detail and sophistication of the 'official' version) operated some form of linear scoring in the second half of the nineteenth century. The result of the Surrey v Middlesex match at The Oval in 1876 was assumed to be a victory by one run for Middlesex, until:

> It was discovered that the scorers had made a mistake and that the match had ended in a tie. Naturally, Middlesex did not accept this decision until due enquiry had been made but nobody questioned the good faith of the scorers, and there seemed no possible room for doubt that a mistake had been made in adding up the numbers the first time. According to a statement in the Cricket Field by Mr. C.W. Alcock 'When the game ended it was thought that Middlesex had won by one run. As it happened, I was keeping the score in the usual way done by the Press and at the fall of the ninth wicket I discovered that the score on the board was wrong. So we sent for the Press books and checked them in the presence of V.E. Walker and I.D. Walker. Press books are kept in such a way that the position of the two batsmen after every run can be traced. We found that a mistake had actually been made and that the result was a tie.' (7)

There have been many variations on the linear method since and a number of first-class and other scorers have designed sheets to their personal taste. The best known today is that designed, used and marketed by Bill Frindall, the BBC's *Test Match Special* scorer. Others record the same or similar information, though not always in the same order.

The standard scoring text book is the late Tom Smith's *Cricket Umpiring and Scoring*, based on the work of its predecessor by R.S. Rait Kerr. Its third edition appeared in 1996, having been revised and updated by the Association of Cricket Umpires and Scorers. Despite the recentness of that revision, linear scoring is given but a passing mention and then not by name, being referred to as 'advanced' scoring. It is advanced only to the extent that it came later – though, as we have seen, not as late as has generally been assumed – and indeed in many ways is more straightforward in that only one entry per ball is required and it is easier to follow the progress of the match and ascertain what the American sporting media call the head-to-head between each batsman and each bowler. It is possible to provide the same information in a traditional scoresheet by using a different colour for each bowler, but, as indicated above, if this method is used, the total balls received, which is the figure more usually required, is less easily calculable.

Derek Hibbs's useful little book *Cricket Scoring* which is and claims to be no more than a handbook for scorers in club cricket, also refers to linear scoring as 'advanced' (8), but largely because it constitutes the Advanced Scorers Examination of ACU & S which requires candidates *inter alia* to transpose information recorded in a traditional system to a linear system and *vice versa*. He does, however, give a brief description of how it works and its usefulness in providing quick-reference information for commentators, not available from the traditional method of scoring. The most detailed explanations of how linear scoring works are by Bill Frindall in his various published scorebooks. (9)

It is a system that is different rather than better and despite its early introduction and the history of its use by Ferguson, its progress and development have not been rapid and owe more to media requirements than to the pioneering spirit of county scorers. In fact, Ferguson used the linear method for the purpose of providing information for the Press, while still maintaining the traditional method for the official record:

> I have made a study of cricket scoring because I was in the unique position of having to earn a living at it. I use a score book of my own design which contains at least twice as much information as any other in the world and, at the conclusion of each day's play, I copy all the important figures into a more orthodox book which is kept as the official record of the tour ...

> My real reason for recording in such a wealth of detail the hundreds of matches at which I have scored was to help out my friends in the press...I always thought it a good idea to look back and discover how many deliveries one particular bowler had sent down to a given batsman. So did the press! (10)

Another of Ferguson's innovations was the scoring chart, which shows the direction of each scoring shot and when later commandeered by the whizzkids of media graphics, becomes the 'wagon wheel' or 'starburst'. His earliest is of Jack Hobbs's 81 for Surrey against the Australians at The Oval in 1912 and, except for the fact that it is hand-drawn rather than computer generated, is no different from the versions used today.

It was not only the Press that found Fergie's statistics and charts helpful and perhaps the difference between him and some later statisticians was that he produced figures in the service of the game, rather than figures for the sake of figures. His *Wisden* obituary records:

> ... figures fascinated him... Besides actual scoring, he kept diagrams of every stroke played and every ball bowled – and who fielded it. Touring captains, including D G Bradman and D R Jardine, employed his charts to study the strengths and weaknesses of the opposing batsmen. (11)

For the compilation of scoring charts, Bill Frindall uses the method of dividing the playing area into nine sectors and numbering them from one to nine anti-clockwise from third man to fine leg. (The Boxill system mentioned below is very similar but uses letters rather than numbers.) Each scoring stroke is then annotated according to the direction in which it is played. While the method may lack the precision of the wagon wheel/starburst method, it at least has the advantage of showing more clearly a batsman's favourite scoring areas and in addition eliminates the mostly abortive work of beginning to prepare a chart for each batsman – abortive, because there is no way of knowing at the beginning of an innings whether it is going to be a world-record-breaking 375 or one streaky inside edge through leg gully.

As radio and television broadcasting became more involved with the game, so linear scoring became more prevalent as Arthur Wrigley, Roy Webber, Jack Price, Michael Fordham and finally Bill Frindall occupied the post of scorer to what eventually became *Test Match Special*. Roy Webber developed his own version (12) with essentially the same advantages as those described by Ferguson, then Bill Frindall refined, firmed up and marketed the system, so that 'the Frindall method' and 'linear scoring' are to an extent in scoring vocabulary interchangeable.

It is somewhat later that linear scoring hits the county scene. Jack Hill, who succeeded Andrew Sandham as Surrey scorer in 1971, used the linear method and there have been a number of variations since, some designed by county scorers and others to satisfy their individual idiosyncrasies. The information recorded is similar, though the order in which it is arranged may vary. The linear system now used by Surrey County Cricket Club is one among several, and experienced scorers find few difficulties in switching between them once they have become accustomed to the layout.

One advantage pointed out by Roy Webber is that the linear system facilitates checking figures and, while it is not my intention in this study to deal extensively with scoring techniques, as that exercise has already been undertaken – at least for the traditional method of scoring – by Smith and Hibbs, it is perhaps worthy of note that the Surrey sheet has provision for balls bowled in the innings, so it is relatively straightforward at any stage to undertake the standard trial balancing check that balls delivered equal balls received parallel to the confirmation that – with appropriate adjustments for extras – runs scored equals runs conceded equals the total score.

In addition to the worksheet, there is a summary sheet which is completed with the usual scorecard details and the Frindall method has a third sheet on which the cumulative bowling figures are kept up to date. Some scorers manage to dispense with the third sheet and work quite happily with the bowling figures on the worksheet. It is personal preference, but for ease of checking the bowling figures I subscribe to the three-sheet method.

The symbols for extras and wickets are identical to those used in traditional scoring, as recommended by the ACU & S – although there are variants in Australia where B, LB, W, NB and X tend to be used rather than △, ▽, X, O and W – and despite the fact that it is spread across three sheets, the system is a good deal easier to work than may at first appear.

The advantages of linear scoring against the traditional method are debatable. It is certainly more convenient to make, but one entry per ball, rather than the time-honoured two to the batsman-two on the accumulator-two against the bowler method, but for most club scorers the traditional method is perfectly adequate and easily understood.

Where linear scoring does come into its own, however, is in its ability to answer questions such as 'How long since Thorpe scored a boundary?' and to provide an instant record of the runs scored and balls faced by each batsman. Such questions may not be significant at club level, or may not require an immediate answer, but, at first-class level, where the Press are requiring such information and certainly in scoring for radio and television, a linear system is indispensable and all county scorers, even when using the traditional method, have at least a skeleton linear system alongside.

The concept of balls faced as a measure of individual and team scoring rates is not exactly new, although its universal acceptance has been slow. *Wisden* still records its fastest hundreds and fastest fifties in terms of minutes rather than balls for the simple reason that, until quite recently, the information was neither available nor readily calculable from the scorebook – even when the scorebook is available.

It is not always possible to trace the progress of a match from the early scorebooks as the overs are not numbered, the bowling analysis does not recognise separate spells, byes and leg byes are marked simply as dots and it is thus impossible to ascertain when the batsman have changed ends. It may not always be clear which batsman faced a particular ball with the result that to the entry on P.G.H. Fender's 35-minute century for Surrey against Northamptonshire in 1920, the Editor is obliged to add a footnote to the effect that research of the scorebook has shown that the hundred was reached in between 40 and 46 balls.

A rapid rate of scoring does put some pressure on the scorers to keep up and this must have been even more the case in 1920 when over rates were about 24 per hour. The Northamptonshire scorebook is the only primary source available (the Surrey ones for the period, as mentioned in the last chapter, are missing) and that has a number of inconsistencies in both the batting and bowling records; for example, the sum of the scoring strokes is 596, yet the Surrey total is recorded as 619 for 5 declared (13), emphasising

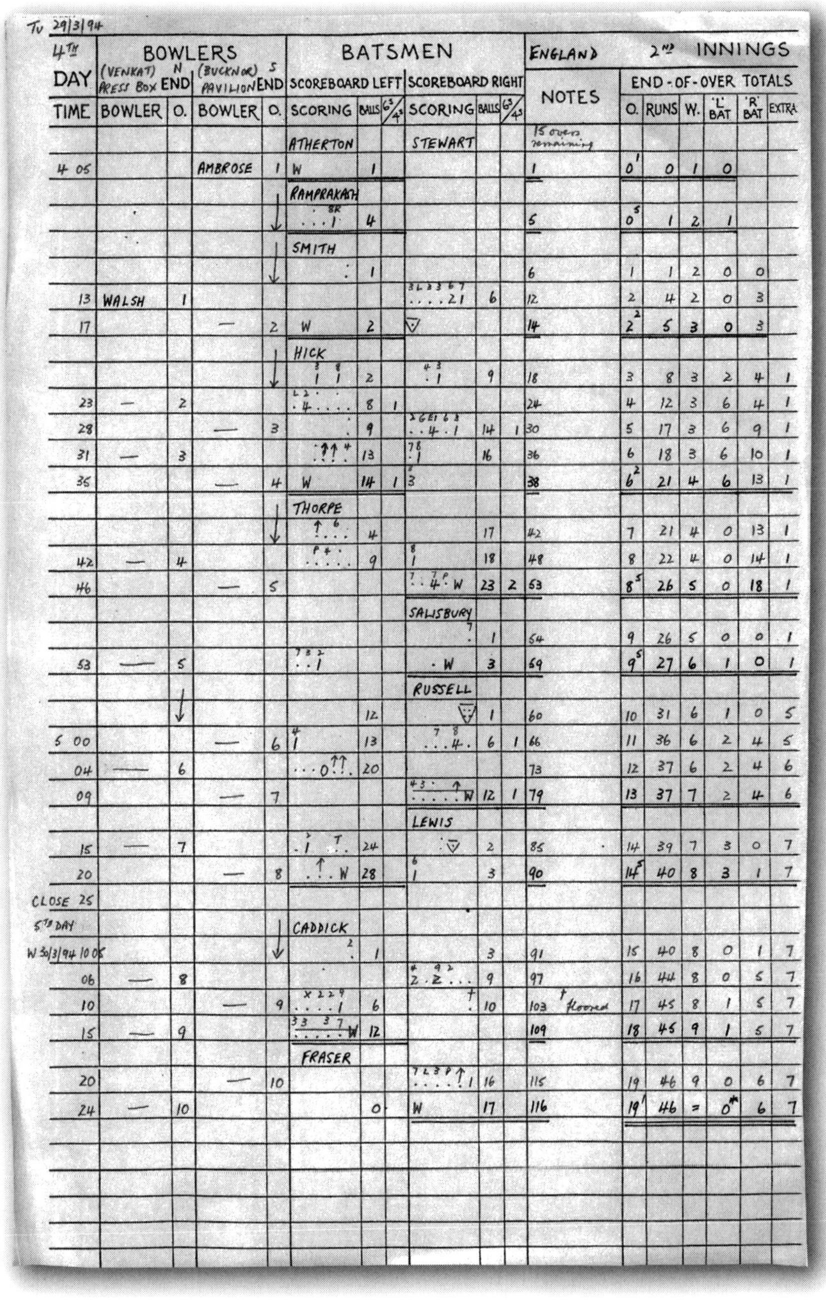

	BOWLERS			BATSMEN				ENGLAND	2ND INNINGS				
4TH DAY	(VENKAT) N PRESS BOX END		(BUCKNOR) S PAVILION END	SCOREBOARD LEFT			SCOREBOARD RIGHT	NOTES	END-OF-OVER TOTALS				
TIME	BOWLER	O.	BOWLER	O.	SCORING	BALLS 6/4	SCORING	BALLS 6/4		O.	RUNS	W.	'L' BAT	'R' BAT	EXTRA

Full scorecard (handwritten, England 2nd innings):

TIME	BOWLER (N end)	O.	BOWLER (S end)	O.	SCOREBOARD LEFT scoring	balls 6/4	SCOREBOARD RIGHT scoring	balls 6/4	NOTES	O.	RUNS	W.	L BAT	R BAT	EXTRA
					ATHERTON		STEWART		15 overs remaining						
4 05			AMBROSE	1	W 1	1			1	0¹	0	1	0		
					RAMPRAKASH ...1	4			5	0⁵	1	2	1		
					SMITH : 1	1			6	1	1	2	0	0	
13	WALSH	1					21	6	12	2	4	2	0	3	
17			—	2	W 2	2	▽		14	2²	5	3	0	3	
					HICK 1 1	2	:1	9	18	3	8	3	2	4	1
23	—	2			.4....	8 1			24	4	12	3	6	4	1
28			—	3		9	..4.1	14 1	30	5	17	3	6	9	1
31	—	3			.??⁴	13	7̇ 1	16	36	6	18	3	6	10	1
35	—			4	W	14 1	3		38	6²	21	4	6	13	1
					THORPE ↑.6...	4		17	42	7	21	4	0	13	1
42	—	4			.?..	9	1	18	48	8	22	4	0	14	1
46	—			5	.4° W	23 2			53	8⁵	26	5	0	18	1
					SALISBURY		1		54	9	26	5	0	0	1
53	—	5			..1		. W	3	59	9⁵	27	6	1	0	1
					RUSSELL	12	▽	1	60	10	31	6	1	0	5
5 00			—	6	1	13	....4.	6 1	66	11	36	6	2	4	5
04	—	6			...0??	20			73	12	37	6	2	4	6
09	—			7			......W	12 1	79	13	37	7	2	4	6
					LEWIS										
15	—	7			.1 .T.	24	▽	2	85	14	39	7	3	0	7
20	—			8	.1.W	28	1	3	90	14⁵	40	8	3	1	7
CLOSE 25															
5TH DAY W 30/3/94 10 05					CADDICK .	1		3	91	15	40	8	0	1	7
06	—	8			.		2.2...	9	97	16	44	8	0	5	7
10			—	9	x..?...1	6	.	10	103 flogged	17	45	8	1	5	7
15	—	9			.....W	12			109	18	45	9	1	5	7
					FRASER										
20			—	10			1	16	115	19	46	9	0	6	7
24	—	10				0	W	17	116	19¹	46	=	0	6	7

First-class innings usually spread over several linear sheets – this particular effort needed only one. England's 46 all out at Port of Spain, Trinidad, 29 & 30 March 1994 [Bill Frindall] once again that it is not always possible to be absolutely categorical about the authenticity of some early records.

The fastest recorded authentic hundred – i.e. disregarding those scored in contrived circumstances to expedite a declaration – is by David Hookes who achieved it in 34 balls. How this compares with earlier efforts by (say) Gilbert Jessop around the turn of the century, who recorded hundreds in 40 and 42 minutes in 1897 and 1907, we do not know and never shall.

Instrumental in crystallising the thinking in the minutes v balls issue was the advent of limited overs cricket and money. When the John Player's County League began in 1969, there was a prize of £250 for the fastest 50. It was won by Keith Boyce who clocked 23 *minutes*. Then, someone, somewhere must have said that the measure of time was less valid than that of balls received and in 1972 the prize went to Glenn Turner who made 50 from 32 *balls*. There was still an element of unfairness in that the prize was restricted to televised matches, but that is another story ...

Bill Ferguson was recording balls received somewhat earlier and in the statistical appendices to Douglas Jardine's book about the 1932–33 'bodyline' tour (14) *In Quest of the Ashes* includes tables of runs scored and balls received by each batsman against each bowler in each Test and over the series.

Roy Webber in the 1950s demonstrates that it is possible to calculate balls received, but does not maintain a cumulative record and the statistic does not form an integral part of the system. It began to do so when Bill Frindall redesigned the Ferguson system in 1966 and for media scoring has done so ever since.

Official records, however, have been slower to catch on. We have seen how limited overs cricket accelerated the inclusion of balls received, but it did not become a feature of first-class records until later. Wisden makes no mention of balls received in Robin Hobbs's 44-minute hundred against the Australians at Chelmsford in 1975 and in The Oval Test match scorebook the first record is as late as 1984. Mike Ringham, who scored for the Australian touring team in 1985 (and two earlier tours), recalls that in that year he was helping county scorers come to terms with the concept of recording balls faced.

The history of the Walter Lawrence Trophy, one of the Ridley Awards, presented for the season's fastest first-class century, parallels the chronology outlined above and illustrates this stuttering progress towards using balls faced rather than time at the crease as a measure of the speed of scoring. Oozing with nostalgia, the list records the first winner as F.E. Woolley with a hundred in 63 minutes for Kent against Northamptonshire at Dover in 1934 and continues to 1939 when L.E.G. Ames recorded one in 70 minutes.

The award then died and was not resurrected until 1966 when it was restricted to Test Matches and calculated in terms of balls (First winner: K.F. Barrington against Australia at Melbourne – 122 balls). It then reverted to all English first-class cricket in 1977 and the speed of scoring was again measured in minutes (As the late Harry Sharp, player and scorer for Middlesex for many years, was fond of reminding his colleagues: 'We didn't have balls in my day!'). Only in 1985 are balls introduced and the first two winners are, perhaps unsurprisingly, I.T. Botham and I.V.A. Richards.

That nostalgic diversion serves to illustrate that, while linear scoring systems have provided the facility to record balls faced for some time and media scorers have used it, it has only recently replaced time batted as the official method of measuring speed of scoring.

Opponents of linear scoring have argued that there is too much to do at the end of an over, especially when a wicket falls on the last ball. It is certainly true that the demands are greater than under the traditional system, but, on the other hand more information is immediately available and there is usually time while the players are changing over to record the information. And the sky will not fall down if the changed statistics resulting from an over with extras, wickets and boundaries to more than one batsman are not entered until half way through the following over.

Most scorers have established a routine of a tripartite check with their colleague of runs from the over, cumulative runs against the bowler and total. Periodically – perhaps every ten overs or so – the batsmen's totals and balls received are compared to ensure that any discrepancies can be rectified before they are continued too far down the sheet. At the Foster's Oval, the almost invariably accurate manual scoreboard is directly opposite the scorebox and any discrepancies in the total and batsmen's scores are usually noticed pretty quickly. The scoreboard operators are among the most efficient in the country, but it is easy enough to miss the umpire's bye or leg-bye signal, especially when it is given in the opposite direction.

Scorers vary as much in their approaches to cross-checking as they do in their personalities: some do no checks at all, preferring to leave it all to the end of the innings; others check at the end of each over. Personally, I prefer to adopt a middle route and check occasionally when the opportunity is available.

There is a certain bonhomie about the county scoring circuit with virtually all scorers on good terms and willing to help one another with cross-checks, calculation of statistics etc. Byron Denning of Glamorgan has a complicated system of numbering the balls of the over by the names of towns running east to west through South Wales – and if that were not sufficiently confusing, he does it in Welsh. I believe the origins of this labyrinthine scheme lie in the coincidence of Porthcawl rhyming with fourth ball and the mythical

2ⁿᵈ INNINGS OF AUSTRALIA — DATE(S) SAT 23 AUG 1997

END VAUXHALL UMPIRE — END PAVILION UMPIRE

TIME	OVER	BOWLER BARKER	BATSMAN TAYLOR	RUNS	6s	4s	BALLS	TOTAL BALLS	BALLS	BATSMAN ELLIOTT	RUNS	6s	4s	BOWLER WILLEY	SCORE	W	B	LB	W	NB	TOTAL

(Handwritten linear-form scorecard of Australia's second innings — batsmen: Taylor, Elliott, Blewett, Waugh M E, Waugh S R, Ponting, Healy, Young, Warne, Kasprowicz, McGrath; bowlers: Barker, Willey, Malcolm, Tufnell; End of over totals recorded.)

TEA 3·41
DRINKS

Australia's second innings in the 1997 Oval Test, this time in linear form

2ⁿᵈ INNINGS OF **AUSTRALIA** DATE(S) **SATURDAY 23 AUGUST** 199 **7**

IN	OUT	MINS	50	100	150	200		BATSMAN	HOW OUT	BOWLER	SCORE	6s	4s	BALLS REC'D
2 33	3 20	47					1	M A TAYLOR	LBW	CADDICK	18		2	34
2 33	2 36	3					2	M T G ELLIOTT	LBW	MALCOLM	4		1	3
2 37	3 34	57					3	G S BLEWETT	c STEWART 1ˢᵗ slip	CADDICK	19		3	36
3 21	3 29	8					4	M E WAUGH	c HUSSAIN 1ˢᵗ slip	TUFNELL	1			7
3 30	4 09	20					5	S R WAUGH	c THORPE	CADDICK	6			19
3 35	4 41	47					6	R T PONTING	LBW	TUFNELL	20		3	35
4 10	4 46	36					7	I A HEALY	c AND B	CADDICK	14		2	17
4 42	(5 24)	42					8	S YOUNG	NOT OUT deep mid-on		4		1	24
4 47	4 55	8					9	S K WARNE	c MARTIN	TUFNELL	3			5
4 56	5 18	22					10	M J KASPROWICZ	c HOLLIOAKE short extra	CADDICK	4			13
5 19	5 24	5					11	G D McGRATH	c THORPE mid-off	TUFNELL	1			2

304·9
295

NEW BALL AT		BYES	3	TOTAL		12	195
SCORE		LEG BYES	4	EXTRAS	10		
OVER		WIDES	1	TOTAL	104	FOR	
TIME/DATE		NO BALLS	2			WICKETS	

FALL OF WICKETS

	1	2	3	4	5	6	7	8	9	10	PLAYING TIME
BATSMAN OUT	2	1	4	3	5	6	7	9	10	11	152
SCORE	5	36	42	49	54	88	92	95	99	104	BALLS BOWLED
BATSMAN NOT OUT	1	3	3	5	6	7	8	8	8	8	193
RUNS ADDED	5	31	6	7	5	32	4	3	4	5	OVER RATE
LENGTH OF PARTNERSHIP MINS	3	43	8	4	15	31	4	8	22	5	12·69
BALLS	4	63	10	6	24	41	7	6	29	5	

52-9
143

BOWLER	OVERS	M	RUNS	WICKETS	WIDES	TOTAL	NO BALLS SCORED OFF	NOT SCORED OFF	TOTAL
MALCOLM	3	-	15	1					
MARTIN	4	-	13	-	1	1			
TUFNELL	13·1	6	27	4				11	2
CADDICK	12	2	42	5					
BYES, LEG BYES			7	—	TOTALS	1		—	2
RUN OUT			—		BALLS BOWLED (EXCLUDING NO BALLS AND WIDES)				193
TOTALS			104	10	BALLS RECEIVED BY BATSMEN				195

	50	100	150	200	250	300	350	400	450		
TIME	3·40	5·20									
OVER	14·4	31·3									
MINS	67	148									

† Actual balls bowled — not runs or extras resulting.   • These figures must agree

Code B

[Reproduced by kind permission of Surrey County Cricket Club]

superstructure has been built on either side. Thus, the first ball is Cas Newydd (Newport), the second Caerdydd (Cardiff), the third Pen-y-Bont (Bridgend), the fifth Castel Nedd (Neath), the sixth Abertawe (Swansea) and the seventh, where there is one, Llanelli. Clem Driver has attempted to devise a rival scheme based on the towns of the Essex coastline, but could find nothing between Clacton and Southend.

Just as runners bore non-runners with talk of courses and PBs, so do scorers bore non-scorers with talk of scoreboxes, their accessibility, the view of the playing area therefrom and the quality of the catering on the grounds of the county circuit. They have even ritualised it and established a 'Standards League'. Until his retirement from the county scene, Bill Petherbridge, Yorkshire's 2nd XI scorer, used to invite scorers to mark on a scale of one to five, the scoring position under accessibility, assistance, communications, comfort and viewpoint and the ground under atmosphere, catering, hospitality, ease of access and car parking.

To revert to linear systems, however, like Topsy, they have just growed and perhaps the time has come when some kind of standardisation should be sought. It may be true, as Emerson reminded us, that a foolish consistency is the hobgoblin of tiny minds and that variety is the spice of life; but just as the ICC has recognised the advantages of standardising the regulations for Limited Overs Internationals, so there are similar advantages in standardising the format in which they are recorded.

The Frindall system is one possibility, but that is designed essentially for radio broadcasting and would have its limitations. An alternative is the system designed by the former Barbados wicket-keeper, Darnley Boxill, which aims to have a space for anything that could possibly happen, including stoppages, missed chances, interval scores, type of bowler, notes on dismissals etc. which, on most other systems, if they are recorded at all, usually take the form of a marginal note.

There were two advantages which I liked when I experimented with the system. One was that, unlike most linear systems, it does have an accumulator which on occasions is helpful. There is no problem working out the total two-thirds of the way through an over if there has been one scoring stroke to add to whatever it was at the beginning of the previous over, but if there has been a no ball which went for two extras, another no ball from which the batsman scored a four, a leg bye, a wide and a three, it is much easier to read the score from an accumulator than to work out that ... er ... 15, I think, are to be added to the score. (15)

The second advantage is that there is a square for each ball and it is thus a little easier to trace the progress of an over, particularly towards the end of a limited overs innings where several quick singles may be completed in rapid succession. It is an advantage that can quickly be negated, however, if there are a number of wides and/or no balls and a ten or eleven-delivery over has to be fitted into six small squares.

There are a number of linear scoring systems around, many of them personal inventions and containing personal idiosyncrasies. Anyone with limited scoring experience can soon find their way round them, but scoring is a service, not to other scorers, but to the players, the Press and the public and it is also important that systems are user-friendly and easily understood by those who wish or need to use them.

In the latter category, of course, are Match Referees in International matches who may need to look at the scoresheets when cogitating about over rates, disciplinary action etc. It would be to their advantage and that of a number of other people if they could look at a scoresheet in Manchester or Madras, Bridgetown or Brisbane and find the information they want in the same place on every sheet they look at. There is a certain amateurish charm in a variety of scoring systems and perhaps a certain degree of dullness in a boring uniformity, but standardised playing regulations for Limited Overs Internationals are now filtering through to domestic competitions and there is sense in standard methods of recording the required statistical information. While the preceding statement is intended to refer to manual methods of scoring, a degree of standardisation is of course already in place in English cricket with the introduction in the last few years of computerised scoring with all scorers using the same methods of recording information on a laptop and transmitting it to a central database. It is to the impact of the technological revolution on the scorebox that we now turn.

Chapter Four

Computerised Scoring

The introduction of laptop computers to county scoreboxes in the last decade of the twentieth century is perhaps less a cause for astonishment than the delay in introducing them. The statistical nature of the game and the fact that a finite number of events can occur from each ball make it an ideal candidate for computerisation. After all, the possibilities, 11 players, 11 ways of being out and 0 – 6 (very occasionally more) runs from each ball are considerably less than those which apply to, for example, chess, bridge or the Treasury's economic model, all of which are speculative rather than factual and fell within IT's ever-increasing ambit some time before our national summer game with the conservatism and inertia that characterises it.

We are, however, no nearer a completely computerised scoring system than we are to the paperless office and, like the transition from notching to pencil and paper or from traditional to linear scoring, there is no clearly defined point at which the written version of the record ceases and the computerised version begins and manual scoring and computerised scoring, for a variety of reasons, not least the reliability of software, seem destined to co-exist as scoring prepares to embark upon its fourth century.

Whether computers are 'better' than scorebooks for ball-by-ball scoring is largely a matter of subjective judgement. For the basic recording of runs, wickets and overs, there is perhaps little to choose between computers, scorebooks and carving notches on sticks. Where the computer does have the advantage, however, is that it eliminates the need for mental arithmetic and constantly updates batting and bowling statistics. In an age when none of us expects to receive hand-written electricity bills or bank statements, perhaps the wonder really is that scorebooks have endured so long.

A few computer whizzkids have written their own programs and invented computerised scorebooks, such as that at Stretford Cricket Club in the Manchester Association, where a prototype system was installed in 1990. It is a keyboard-operated system, designed as far as possible so that the method of entry replicates that of the scorebook e.g. '.', 'X', 'W', etc. The system is also linked to an electronic scoreboard, drives monitor screens in the changing rooms and bars and provides supplementary information in the form of run rates, bar graphs and 'worm' charts. (1)

The computer takeover of the official record of the first-class game, however, came in 1991 with the introduction of the Broadsystem, the frying-pan for many county scorers, though only retrospectively did they recognise it as such when they were forced into the fire of 1993 and what subsequently became 'Cricket Record'.

What is believed to be the first 'professional' computerised cricket scoring system was developed by Dr Jim Briggs, formerly of the Department of Computer Science at the University of York, in the winter of 1983–84, at the request of Leeds Rugby League Club, the owners of Headingley Cricket Ground. So, just as overarm bowling has its origins in early nineteenth century fashion (John Willes's sister being unable to bowl underarm because of the width of her crinoline), so computerised cricket scoring has its origins in rugby league!

The result was a new piece of software, CSP (Cricket Scoring Program), a computerised scorebook with modules enabling it to drive *inter alia*, the Headingley cricket scoreboard. Two years later, Dr Briggs was approached by a company based in France (a source less likely than crinolines or rugby league as a pioneer of cricketing innovation), PariSportinfo to produce a modified version of CSP to enable it to send information down a telephone line to be converted into synthesised speech. The result was a system which hit the market in 1991 under the name Cricketscene and conveyed to cricket enthusiasts dialling an 0891 number provided by Broadsystem Ltd an oral representation of the latest score from the ground of their choice from information supplied by first-class county scorers. The uptake by the public was, however, insufficient, and Broadsystem pulled out at the end of the 1991 season leaving the way clear for the Press Association, the TCCB and 'Cricket Record'.

The main commercial purpose is to supply an accurate and up-to-date score to the Press Association whence it is distributed to sections of the media such as Ceefax, Teletext, regional and national newspapers and the Internet. Consequently, any mistake has the potential for being repeated about 100 million times! It is now beginning to work after severe teething problems in its early days when 'nightmarish' and 'nonsensical' were among the more polite epithets used by county scorers to describe it. There is still scope for improvement and we are nowhere near the end of the road which leads to a perfect and infallible cricket scoring system, but from the sharp knife and hazel stick to mouse and hard disk we have progressed a considerable way along it.

The system had an initial capital cost of £140,000 and originated in an agreement between Computer Newspaper Services (CNS), a wholly-owned subsidiary of the Press Association, and the TCCB. Announced in early 1993 after trials at Durham and Nottingham the previous summer, improving the lot of the county scorer did not feature on the list of reasons for its introduction. The rationale was to replace the traditional method of conveying the score to the media by having staff or freelance reporters telephoning their newspapers at half-hourly intervals by the transmission of information – still by telephone line but in electronic data rather than by voice – to a central database at CNS headquarters at Howden, near Goole, whence it was the intention to transmit it to the Press Association, Ceefax, Teletext, overseas agencies and later the Internet.

County scorers, most of whom had left school if not before Babbage invented his difference engine, then certainly before computers were such an integral part of day-to-day existence, were provided with minimal training and required to operate the system from the following April. Despite the confidence of CNS that most of the bugs had been removed from the program, (2) its early days were not an unqualified success. Its introduction on 14 April 1993 amid the frosts of an English spring into scoreboxes at Fenner's and The Parks was accompanied by curious journalists and other interested parties in far greater numbers than occupied the public benches at the traditional start to the season. Ivo Tennant reported in *The Times*:

> In most senses it was a typical spring day at Fenner's: lots of sweaters, plenty of runs from the visiting batsmen and keen out-cricket by the undergraduates. In one sense it differed. A lap-top computer was in use in the scorers' box, not without some difficulty since the hamburger van was operating off the same power circuit ...

A few weeks down the line, other problems had been identified and journalists were pointing the finger at TCCB who were guaranteed a minimum of £40,000 from CNS for the sell-out:

> Not a product of the Murray Report, more a product of TCCB officials' determination to push through their own ideas regardless. It is no longer possible to ask a county scorer how he is, because he will tell you, at length, or perhaps involve you in a discussion about whether it takes nine computer moves to record a stumping off a wide, or 13. Many scorers are now doing two jobs, fighting the technology by day and writing up the scorebook at night.

Teething troubles? Perhaps. But the whole concept was flawed. The TCCB believed that this method would get scores through to the newspapers faster and encourage evening papers to devote more space to cricket. Many, if not most, 'evening' papers now have final deadlines too early to get any cricket at all. (3)

As the season progressed some weird idiosyncrasies began to emerge. Batsmen were assumed to lose their wickets in the same order as their names appeared on the scorecard, run outs were credited to the bowler, a stroke indicated on the radial scoring chart as sending the ball beyond the boundary caused the total to revert to zero and the addition of 128 overs to the bowling statistics every time a wide was entered produced some surreal bowling figures.

One difficulty, remedied a year later, was the laborious method of correcting errors, which involved calling up a separate match history program, finding the correct innings, over and ball and superimposing the correct entry. By the time the correction had been made, the match had already moved on a couple of overs and 'going into history' became one of the catch phrases of the summer of 1993. It is rumoured that one scorer, when his county was playing the Zimbabwean touring team, was so far into history that when he actually returned to the current file, the opponents came up as Southern Rhodesia.

Notwithstanding all this, whether the information stored and transmitted was accurate – or, more usually, widely adrift – became of little relevance, as on those few days on which the sun condescended to make an appearance, it disappeared entirely from the laptop screen. Add to all this that 'going into history' left scorers at least an over behind the actual play and it will be deduced that stress levels were fairly high and their language reminiscent of that with which the Australian tourists impressed a number of match referees that summer.

The main criticisms were not so much of the principles of computerised scoring as of its over-rapid introduction with limited consultation and minimal preparation. Michael Blumberg, Editor of *Cricket World* was less than gruntled and compared the exercise with the imposition of inappropriate computer packages on commerce and industry 20 – 30 years earlier.

I have watched with a fair measure of incredulity the crass mismanagement of the introduction of TCCB's computer scoring package. Rushed into implementation with a fraction of the 'promised training' this fiasco has all the characteristics of those examples from the 1960s and 1970s I have mentioned.

Here we have 'fat cat' consultants, imposing a system on a largely computer illiterate TCCB with all those predictably comic pitfalls. Cost savings which prove illusory, an arrogance towards 'minions' that actually do score – 'Throw your scorebooks away', an arrogance towards that very body which includes highly skilled mathematicians, statisticians, computer programmers and old fashioned scorers, namely the Association of Cricket Statisticians. It is a matter of record that those responsible for the computer scoring package and its introduction consulted neither the ACS nor the Association of Umpires and Scorers nor for that matter the Cricket Writers Club which has a number of county and professional scorers as members. Indeed TCCB is on record as stating 'It is TCCB's right and responsibility to run First-Class, Test and County Cricket as it likes and therefore how it decides to carry out scoring is its business alone and nothing to do with ACS (or ACU and S). (4)

The controversy raged on through the summer of 1993 and was polarised in the pages of *Wisden* the following spring. Bill Frindall who knows a thing or two about scoring and statistics wrote:

In checking the domestic first-class scores for this almanack, I maintain close contact with the scorers and could fill several pages with quotes from their correspondence to illustrate the frustration and despair which they suffered. The friendly atmosphere of the scorebox with its rich banter was totally destroyed. The only tangible product of this innovation was a vast increase in the number of scoring errors and differences in the two records of the same match, the last of which was not unravelled until two months after the season ended. This was a system conceived without sufficient planning and foisted on the counties without due consideration for the welfare of those compelled to operate it. The fabric of our professional game is being whittled away by mindless opportunism.

One lesson should have been learnt from this chaos. Any mechanised system of scoring a cricket match must be supported by a manuscript record. Not only is this essential to fall back on when the machine (or its operator) breaks down, but is vital to the continuity of cricket's archives. (5)

Ken Lawrence, Media Relations Manager for the TCCB at the time, while conceding that the introduction of computerised scoring was a troubled one, pointed to the Press Association's tighter grip on CNS and its assurances that all requirements would be satisfied in the second summer of operation and went on to emphasise the improved service to the media and the spin-offs of generating more information which might be used for coaching purposes. (6)

CNS became PA Data Design and having virtually completed the development work the following summer, in October 1994, ceded the management of 'Cricket Record' to PA Sport, based in Leeds, just beyond the former northern extremity of the M1.

Since those early days, matters have improved gradually to the point where by the 1996 season the vast majority of errors were operator- rather than computer-generated. Some information is entered via a keyboard, but the majority owes its generation to a mouse being shuffled round a mat and clicked. Entries are made on a schematic representation of the field for the direction of a batsman's stroke, for the number of runs scored and for the method of dismissal when he is out, and software computes the rest from there, changing batting statistics and bowling figures, generating a traditional innings scorecard, a match scorecard, traditional scorebook and a 'starburst' for each batsman. Further, each county receives weekly from PA Sport, usually accurate batting and bowling averages and related statistics for the four main competitions.

The amount of equipment associated with the system has mushroomed. The exercise started with a laptop and a mouse; during the 1993 season, an external modem was added to supplement, or effectively substitute for, the non-operational internal one. The problem of the illegibility of the screen was solved by the installation of monitors. Printers came on the scene in 1994, as, 12 months late, did operating manuals and, finally, mobile phones were supplied to those counties with no telephonic communication in the scorebox and/or outgrounds with limited contact with the rest of the world .

So the boots of scorers' cars are carrying almost as much equipment as those of the players, scoreboxes at times resemble electricians' workshops and time is inevitably spent at the beginning and end of play setting up and dismantling divers electrical circuits. On Test grounds and the major county grounds it is quite feasible to set up the gear and leave it in place for the duration of the match, but on outgrounds where the scoring facility is often a caravan or a tent, security demands that this quite expensive equipment is removed at close of play each day. No wonder that scorers quietly yearn for the days when all they had to do was arrive five minutes before the start of play and carve themselves a branch or two from the nearest hazel tree.

By the end of 1997, however, the nightmare scenario was over. A lot of hard work by scorers and PA technicians produced a system that was working and providing thousands of Ceefax and Teletext viewers and millions of Internet surfers with accurate and up-to-date scores of first-class cricket matches.

But then in 1998, it all went pear-shaped again. New Windows 95 software was introduced and, like the second-hand sports car bought from an unscrupulous dealer by Harold Steptoe and resold a week later at a markedly lower price, there were all kinds of things wrong with it that weren't wrong with it before. It was some consolation that the screen display was now in colour, so the mistakes showed up with increased clarity. However, bit by bit and byte by byte, the system was cajoled into a kind of working order. At the end of the season it was working tolerably well and by the start of the 1999 season the whizzkids had ironed out most of the remaining wrinkles. They needed to: 1999 being World Cup Year and the information passing down the telephone wires from the laptops generating more interest than Derbyshire v Northants on a wet Thursday.

There can be little doubt, therefore, that computers in the scorebox are here to stay and will improve with advancing technology and, as Ken Lawrence indicated in his 1994 *Wisden* article, there are many possibilities beyond the immediate scoring of the match, such as the analysis of where a batsman scores his runs. Its use would be increased if information on the line and length of the balls from which they had been scored were also available and if starbursts could be produced of where bowlers conceded runs as well as where batsmen scored them. By 1999 'Cricket Record' was capable of providing the last-mentioned information, but it is still more limited than some other systems.

One such is 'Cricket Wizard', developed in South Africa by Frikkie Botha who combined his expertise as a computer programmer with his wife's occupation as scorer to the Northern Transvaal Cricket Union at Centurion Park. The system can be used as a pure scoring system to record the basic scoring information, but is also capable of providing additional information and providing it more quickly than does 'Cricket Record' – for example details of bowling analysis per spell, partnership details in terms of runs, minutes, balls and the contribution of each batsman, scoring rates, balls per fifty runs, run rate for each five overs.

The 'wagon wheel' information is akin to the Frindall system of dividing the playing area into segments and indicating the runs scored in each, but instead of nine segments, the choice is six or twenty and the system will provide information for each batsman, for each bowler and for each batsman against each bowler. It is also possible to analyse where the bowler pitches his deliveries (there is a choice of twenty-one areas – seven lengths and three directions), but as yet only for each match and not cumulatively.

The information is used by Bob Woolmer, coach of the South African national side, Duncan Fletcher, coach of Western Province and South Africa 'A' and Desmond Haynes, former coach of Sussex County Cricket Club. Woolmer, in fact, gives examples of how he used the resulting charts on England's 1995–96 tour of South Africa to demonstrate both Michael

Atherton's ability to deal with the straight ball and his vulnerability to deliveries just short of a length and just outside off stump. So a fifth slip/second gully became a regular – and successful – field placing. With Graeme Hick the reverse was the case: balls wide of the off stump, he treated as four-balls, but tight bowling curbed his profligacy for boundaries, resulted in his hitting in the air and led to his being caught at mid-wicket from a full toss. (7)

Scientific and systematic analysis of the opposition is not new on the coaching scene: generating the information by computer *is* and the strong likelihood is that it can only increase.

So far, the computerisation of the scorebook, the scoreboard and improved technology for printing scorecards have developed separately, but there is no reason why it should be ever thus. It is virtually certain that computerised scoring systems, their initial teething troubles behind them, will continue to provide more information of greater accuracy and at greater speed, but there is no reason why the same program should not drive both scorecard and scoreboard, so that the spectator has the advantage of seeing a version of what is in the computerised scorebook without the necessity of an intermediate scoreboard operator. Similarly, if cricket-watchers still feel the need for a printed scorecard with the up-to-date position, then it should be no problem to provide at strategic points around the ground coin-in-the-slot machines which for 50p or whatever (or doubtless, by the time they are installed, the equivalent in euros) would satisfy (albeit temporarily) their insatiable desire for more and better statistical information.

Chapter Five

So ... What Do Scorers Do?

Although scorers and their antecedent notchers had been around since at least the beginning of the eighteenth century, it was not until the end of the nineteenth that they made their appearance in the Laws of Cricket and not until the 1947 Code that they are considered worthy of more than a passing reference.

The 1884 Code, which represented a complete revision provided that 'Any run or runs so scored shall be duly recorded by the scorers appointed for the purpose' and give or take a bit of stylistic tidying up and the omission of the pseudo-legalistic but ultimately meaningless 'duly', that provision has remained virtually unchanged until the present day.

The M C C had drawn up its 'Instructions to Umpires' in 1892 and in 1901 added to it a 'Code of Signalling' which provided that:

Umpires should wait until a signal has been answered by the scorer before allowing the game to proceed.

In 1920, those same instructions were expanded to give further acknowledgement to the presence of scorers, but rather like the Ten Commandments, the emphasis is on what thou shalt not do rather than what thou shalt.

There, for the next two decades, amid indigestible verbiage about sides fielding with ten men or less, obstacles within the boundary and the luncheon interval, we find that: 'It is not the scorers' business to dictate to the Umpire. The Umpire should direct the scorer what to record.'

There was a subtle change in 1934 when *scorers'* suddenly becomes *scorer's*, although whether the amendment is legality recognising reality, a semantic adjustment to ensure consistency with the following sentence or simply a typesetter's aberration is unclear.

Perhaps it is simply a reflection of the 1930s Depression. The amendment is certainly consistent with the Rules issued by the Board of Control for Test Matches which provided in 1930 that the *scorers* should be paid £10 per Test Match and for the next three years that the *scorer* should be paid £5.

In 1939, however, with a major revision of the Laws of Cricket by MCC, the status of scorers receives an marginal upgrade in that as well as being obliged to record the runs under Law 2, the prohibition on their dictating to the umpires becomes enshrined as note (f) to Law 3. There is also a slight amendment in that 'should' moves from the semi-optional to the mandatory and becomes 'shall'.

However, the erstwhile 'Notes and Instructions to Umpires' are now 'Notes for Scorers and Umpires' (albeit, after the separate Laws for One-Day Matches and supplementary Laws for Single Wicket), acknowledge again that there may be more than one scorer and, somewhat less curtly than their predecessors, provide:

1. (a) The scorers must accept the umpires' signals and instructions, and though it is no part of their duty to dictate to the umpires, mutual consultation to clear up doubtful points is at all times permissible.

(b) During the progress of the game, if two scorers have been appointed, they should frequently check the total to ensure that the score sheets agree.

(c) The umpires should wait until a signal has been answered by the scorer before allowing the game to proceed ...

There is then a sub section on the recommended method of entering No Balls and Wides in the score sheet, the first acknowledgement in the Notes of the existence of the latter.

The post-war codification of 1947, recognising changes in society and the disappearance from English hymnology of the rich man in his castle and the poor man at his gate sees a major advance in the legal status of scorers in that they now appear in the very first line '(A) THE PLAYERS, UMPIRES AND SCORERS' and they have their own Law which provides for their recording runs, accepting and acknowledging umpires' instructions and signals and permits consultation with umpires on doubtful points.

The scorebook now makes its first appearance with instructions as to how to record in it the dismissal of batsmen given out Handled the Ball, Hit the Ball Twice, Obstructing the Field or Run Out.

The Notes for Scorers and Umpires (One-Day Matches and Single Wicket have now been expunged) have been modified to cross-refer to the new Law 4, but the combined practical effect of Law 4 and the Notes stays the same.

And so things remained until the next major codification of the Laws in 1980 when the material which was previously included in Notes now became enshrined in the Laws.

Notwithstanding, however, the gradual enhancement of the scorer's status under the Laws over the preceding 80 years, the function is still dealt with in a fairly cursory fashion in Law 4 of the current Laws of Cricket, which, sandwiched between Law 3 which deals with the Umpires and Law 5 which deals with the Ball, states in terms of stark simplicity:

1. Recording Runs
All runs shall be recorded by scorers appointed for the purpose. Where there are two scorers they shall check frequently to ensure that the score-sheets agree.

2. Acknowledging Signals
The scorers shall accept and immediately acknowledge all instructions given to them by the umpires.

And that's it. No legal obligation even to record wickets, let alone provide captain and coach with lunch-time bowling figures or supply instant information to the Press of the minutes, balls, fours and sixes included in Bloggs's umpteenth century for the county.

There are other direct references to scorers in Law 3 which *inter alia* continue the previous provision that the umpires will wait until a signal has been acknowledged before allowing play to proceed (3.13). However, consultation between scorers and umpires over doubtful points is now 'essential', rather than, as previously, permissible.

The remaining direct reference is in Law 21.7, Acceptance of the Result, which deals with accepting the scores as *notified* by the scorers and *accepted* by the umpires. Let it be noted, however, that this Law marks a shift of responsibility. In the 1947 Code, neither scorers, nor umpires received any recognition as far as the result of the match was concerned. The responsibility of satisfying themselves on the correctness of the scores rested entirely with the captains.

The responsibility for the correctness of the result under Law 21.6 lies with the umpires and not the scorers, as does the responsibility for 'satisfying themselves on the correctness of the scores throughout and at the conclusion of the match' (Law 3.14). The Laws are silent on the methods by which umpires are expected to fulfil these responsibilities and the conscientiousness of the men in white coats in observing these obligations varies tremendously. Some are oblivious to or choose to ignore their obligations, while at the other extreme, some club umpires take on to the field with them a gadget similar to those used for counting rows of knitting and check it against the scorebook at intervals and again at the end of play.

Umpires on the first-class circuit, however, tend to take the view that the scorers will get it right, that although the scoreboard will on occasion be incorrect, the scoresheet will reflect the state of play. In my brief time on the county circuit I have never known an umpire attempt to check the accuracy of the scoresheet.

Former first-class umpire Don Oslear takes the view that there is no way an umpire can do what is already an onerous job and simultaneously be responsible for the accuracy of the score, but this view failed to carry any weight when he was asked to comment on the final draft of the 1980 Code. (1)

Other references to the Scorers in the Laws are more oblique: the Laws dealing with the correctness of the scores pre supppose their existence and in particular Law 21.6 acknowledges the possibility of a mistake in scoring. Umpires may miscount (Law 22.4), be in doubt (Law 27.4) and change their decision (Law 27.6), but only scorers can make mistakes.

Principally, however, although scorers can and do make mistakes and plenty of them, they are still – subject legally to the overall jurisdiction of the umpires – the guardians of the official and correct version of the match and are right even when they are wrong. At any first-class fixture of any significance there are numbers of 'amateur' scorers keeping their own version of the match, as well as media scorers doing the same. These versions may vary, if only in minor detail, but it has always been conventional wisdom that there can only be one official version and that is the one kept and agreed by the 'official' scorers. Not that the latter are complacent or unprepared to accept advice – and the scorebox on some county grounds is so positioned that they often have no alternative but to seek an opinion from the Press, scoreboard operators or the nearest fielder or spectator on, for example, the identity of a catcher who may not be within the field of vision – but ultimately, it is the only system which works and any other would cause subsequent statistical chaos.

Even the first recorded tie was really a win by one run. In 1783 Hampshire scored 140 and 62 against Kent's 111 and 91, 202-all by any conventional arithmetic. Haygarth, however, records in *Scores and Biographies*:

A tie match, and the first on record... Kent actually won the match. It was discovered afterwards that Pratt, the scorer whose method (which was the usual one at the time) was to cut a notch on a stick for every run, and to cut every tenth notch longer, in order to count the whole more expeditiously, had, by mistake, marked in one place the eleventh notch instead of the tenth. The stick was

afterwards produced; but the other scorer could not or would not produce his."
(2)

I am aware of only one first-class match where the result has been changed because of a mistake in the scoring (Middlesex v Surrey in 1876 – see Chapter Three), though since before the advent of visual recording of matches, there was no way of verifying that the scorebook actually reflected what went on on the field of play, we can never be absolutely certain, but there are numerous examples of mistakes affecting the official records.

One which has become almost legendary is the Sutcliffe–Holmes (then) record opening partnership of 555 at Leyton in 1932 when Sutcliffe, believing the previous record of 554 to have been broken, threw his wicket away. Whatever was on the scoreboard, the scorebook totalled to 554 and the umpires and scorers were obliged to 'remember' a no ball.

In January 1999 in a Test Match against India in Gwalior, Pakistani batsman Inzamam-ul-Haq had his score adjusted from the 98 not out originally recorded on the official scoresheet to the erroneous 100 not out shown on the scoreboard which had been instrumental in his captain's decision to declare the innings closed.

Dr Vasant Naik, Vice-President of the Association of Cricket Statisticians and Scorers of India, has collected a number of examples of differences in scorers' records (3). For example, in England's then record 903-7 dec at The Oval in 1938, Edrich was c Hassett b O'Reilly in the media and in *Wisden* and lbw b O'Reilly in both official scorebooks. The umpire's recollection was c Hassett, that of a spectator that Edrich was plumb LBW misreading O'Reilly's 'wrong un': there was clearly an element of doubt, as Ferguson's linear sheet has 'Edrich' written in the margin, possibly as a reminder to check the actual method of dismissal with the umpire. Notwithstanding all that, the official version remains LBW.

Dr Naik also points to a delay of 27 years in bringing into line with the official version the individual scores of Alan Watkins and Derek Shackleton (there was a one-run discrepancy) in the New Delhi Test of 1951–52. The correction of Boyle's bowling figures in the 1880 Oval Test, however, took far longer than that. They were still wrong in 1965, but correct by 1978 (see Chapter Two).

Most, if not all, professional scorers have their share of amateur personal or postal questioners anxious to get an official view on their own scoring. The majority are polite and courteous, but some are vindictive and keen to challenge the accuracy of the official score. Fergie was not without his share and relates his experience on his first tour of England in what Dr Naik has called 'the petticoat controversy':

As the tour progressed, I became more and more confident of my scoring ability, being complimented on my books by everyone with the exception of one of the three ladies on tour with us, Mrs Clem Hill. For reasons best known to herself, Mrs Hill also used to keep the score!

At the end of each day's play, she invariably badgered her husband with the complaint that there had been scoring mistakes – just because my books did not agree with the ones she kept for amusement. Clem would look at his wife indulgently and then appeal to me, 'For goodness sake, Fergie, check the wife's book. She insists you're wrong, but I can't be bothered with it.' Perhaps there is something to be said for the countries which impose a strict ban on wives travelling with the cricketers! (4)

Not only in the development of linear scoring was Fergie ahead of his time. Wives and girlfriends were banned from accompanying the England party on their tour to Zimbabwe and New Zealand in 1996–97.

There are more recent examples of scoring discrepancies. Within my own experience, the media scores of a Limited Overs International in Trinidad have differed from the official version, the media being convinced that a run was completed before a run out and the official scorers believing otherwise and there are at least three versions of the number of balls faced by Brian Lara in his record 375; but in each case, the official version is the one that has passed into the record books. (5) (6)

One obvious cause of discrepancy in recording the number of balls faced arises from the different conventions used by media scorers and official scorers when the umpire miscounts the number of balls in an over. Media scorers record the actual number of balls faced and official scorers either delete or invent a ball (It has to be a dot ball and the camouflage is ineffective when there is no dot in any of the seven balls of a six-ball over). The practice is contrary to the teaching of the Association of Cricket Umpires and Scorers and cannot be justified in terms of statistical accuracy. Its only defence is that it saves the umpires from a mild degree of embarrassment.

My own method for matches where such details as balls faced are published in the media is to follow the party line on five- and seven-ball overs (I have not yet experienced fewer than five or more than seven, but neither is impossible) and make a marginal note of the differences and reasons for them.

However, although the Laws may give the impression that the contribution of the scorers to a match is limited to recording runs, acknowledging signals and making mistakes, it is implicit that they do other things as well. Although there is no specific provision in Law 4 for recording wickets, they are reminded, as they were in the 1947 version of those methods of dismissal for which the bowler does not get credit, and to add the new 'Timed Out'.

Thus, just as society believes that doctors will not limit their activities to a straight observation of the Hippocratic oath, so society – or at least that part of it which takes an interest in cricket – will assume that scorers will do things beyond the narrow limits of their obligations under the Laws.

There is an anecdote about a board meeting of an industrial concern in a northern city. The accountant ventured an opinion on some matter of policy to be shrivelled to his appropriate size by the Chairman with the harrowing and direct comment: 'Shurrup, thee, tha's nobbut t'scorer'. What this story may tell us about the view of accountants taken by chairmen of northern industrial organisations is beyond the scope of this book, but it does tell us something about the low esteem in which scorers are generally held.

The scorer is not in a position to influence play. Players do so by playing well or badly, by making runs or taking wickets or catches; umpires should not do so, but may well do so by making an incorrect decision which has a bearing on the play and may well influence the result. Yet, of the three, the scorer is least able to relax his (or her) vigilance. He (or she – and I shall refer to the scorer as 'he' throughout the remainder of this book, recognising that it is politically incorrect as there are a number of lady scorers around, but the majority are male and I do so simply for semantic convenience) then must watch every ball and continue to do so until the ball has become dead, acknowledge any signal from the umpire and then begin the whole process again, repeating it 1,000 times or more in the course of an innings, perhaps 100,000 in the course of a season.

Umpires will argue that they must be equally vigilant and concentrate on every ball. True enough, but they know that they will not be required to adjudicate on an LBW appeal while standing at the striker's end or a hit wicket at the non-striker's end, so to that extent can 'switch off' from certain decisions: but the scorer must be prepared to record any number of runs, any number of extras and any one of nine ways of being out (eleven, if 'timed out' and 'retired out' are included, although by definition a ball is not required for those).

So, having seen the legal status of scorers evolve from the unrecognised, through very low to slightly less low, we must now ask 'What do scorers do?' and the answer is that they provide a service. To whom? To anyone with a direct or indirect interest in the game. Certainly to players, umpires, spectators and, for scorers on the county, minor county and major club circuits, to the media and via that route, to newspaper and magazine readers, Ceefax and Teletext followers and, since the recent link-up of Cricket Record, to some 100 million surfers on the Internet.

What I write here of course refers mainly to scorers on the county scene as that is the area with which I am most familiar, but I would not wish to imply that club scorers do not have obligations above and beyond those prescribed by the Laws. They do and fulfil them for the most part voluntarily, unpaid and in their own time.

The first and immediate obligation is to players, umpires and spectators on the ground – in that order of importance. All need to be kept informed of the state of play through the medium of the scoreboard, the information contained on which can vary from runs and wickets on a few rusty tin plates hung on even rustier nails on the village green to the latest bowling figures, scoring rates achieved and scoring rates required on the latest state-of-the-art electronic scoreboards.

In many club, village and even Minor County and County 2nd XI matches, the scorer and scoreboard operator are one and the same, but on the first class circuit, where the functions are separate, the responsibility for the accuracy of what is shown is that of the scorers and where the scorers and scoreboard operators are geographically separated, the responsibility for the accuracy of the score remains with the scorer.

Technically and legally, of course, all that is required is that the runs recorded on the scoresheet are correct, but as the interested parties do not have access to that document, it is of precious little use to anyone if the scoresheets are correct, but the score on the board misleadingly incorrect. The evolution of the scoreboard and the variety of detail shown are covered in Chapters Eight and Nine, but for the moment, it is sufficient to reiterate that the scorers are ultimately responsible for what is shown on it.

In first-class matches, there is also a fairly tight relationship between the scorers and the Press. On some grounds, the Press have their own resident scorer, but even there, confirmation of the correct scores is usually required from the official scorer – and just as umpires are right even when they are wrong, so the score notified by the official scorers is correct even when it is wrong, except in those cases, when under Law 3.14, the umpires may take an alternative view. The Press usually wish to know details of 50s, 100s and multiples thereof in terms of minutes, balls, sixes and fours; at the end of the innings they will require bowling figures and an analysis of extras. Many are better equipped than scorers with career statistics and historical information and are happy to provide it where an announcement via the public address system would be of interest to spectators.

The relationship between the scorers and the public address is also a fairly close one. Indeed, at some counties, the home scorer has the dual responsibility of scoring the match and keeping the spectators informed and entertained. At Glamorgan, Byron Denning's soft Welsh lilt produces a lightness of touch which more often than not hits the right note, such as, on a dull and damp morning with a particularly low attendance: 'Good morning to both of you' or, on the occasion of particularly heavy scoring against Glamorgan: 'Please could parents with young children cover the ears of their offspring as the Glamorgan bowling figures may shock them.'

There will always be disagreements about the kind of information to be transmitted over the PA. In days of increasing commercialisation, there is no way we can avoid welcoming sponsors, announcing benefit events and giving details of T-shirt and book bargains in the county shop; but how much information should be given on the actual cricket? Just as members and spectators vary in their expectations, so counties vary in their practices, some giving no information at all, others announcing every bowling change.

My own view, for what it is worth is that a middle course should be steered, giving information relevant to the match that the spectators cannot see for themselves either on the field of play or on the scoreboard. For instance, if in the final session of play, Joey Benjamin comes on for his fifth bowling spell, his name on one scoreboard and his scorecard number on the other, then there is little point in over-egging the pudding by announcing to the faithful 'Change of bowling at the Vauxhall end ... Joey Benjamin'. On the other hand, it may be of interest to point out that Stewart's century was reached from x balls in y minutes and included a six and however many fours.

There are, however, limits: personally, I would not be interested to know that this is a record fourth-wicket partnership against Derbyshire at The Oval. Today's partnership is relevant in the context of this innings, this match and current circumstances: the fact that some other pair may have done something apparently similar in a different innings in a different match in totally different circumstances is only remotely relevant. But I am a scorer rather than a statistician and not all statisticians, nor indeed all scorers would agree with me.

As well as providing a service for the public, however, the scorer also provides information for the coach and captain. The extent and importance of it can vary, but it is traditional to provide up-to-date bowling figures at intervals, at the close of play and at the conclusion of an innings. Until recently, this has been done by providing a 'bowling slip' but with the advent of the computerised PA Cricket Record, it is now easier to press the appropriate button and generate a computer printout. It is also arithmetically more accurate and provides more information, for example the full scorecard to date. What it does not do, however, is provide information on the over rate, a vexed issue whose importance increases as the season advances, because money – or, to be more precise, the withdrawal of it – is affected by the outcome.

The target over rate in 1995 was 18.5 per hour over the season after allowing three minutes for every wicket taken, four minutes for every drinks interval and whatever time umpires were prepared to allow for injuries, stoppages, sight screen moving, pitch invasions etc. etc. There was a fine of £4,000 for failing to reach the target and an additional £2,000 for every 0.5 of an over below 18, the fine being split evenly between the club and the players. The same rules had applied in 1993 and 1994 when, based on scorers' returns, a number of county clubs had over rates of just over 18.5. The Test and County Cricket Board began to suspect an element of creative arithmetic and in 1995, umpires were asked to submit an independent record of the lengths of sessions and time allowed for stoppages. The result was that more counties were fined. Surrey, having been in the 18.5 and a bit category for the previous two seasons, pulled back to 17.07 from a mid-season low of not much above 16.5 and were fined £8,000.

As one of the players said, professional cricket must be the only job where you have to work overtime to achieve a target and then have pay deducted.

A number of counties were in a similar position and a consequence was that the TCCB in their collective wisdom decided – and, indeed might have done so earlier, had clubs not been so keen to manipulate the figures to avoid fines – that 18.5 was unrealistic and reduced the target to 16 for 1996, but with no time for wickets and drinks intervals. There were innings when no spinners were used and when wickets fell regularly to pace bowlers when 16 overs per hour was difficult to achieve, but the general view was that over a season, the target rate was not unreasonable and most counties now manage to achieve it.

So much for over rates, a relatively insignificant statistic in the plethora that cricket by its nature produces, but one which assumes a disproportionate importance, because of the financial implications associated with it.

Among the more immediate information that scorers are required to provide is the revised target and overs remaining in rain-affected limited overs matches. Before 1997 the calculation was the responsibility of the umpires in conjunction with the Match Manager each club was obliged to appoint for each limited overs match, but in practice the actual calculation was usually that of the scorers with, in many cases, the home scorer acting as Match Manager. The calculation in English cricket was a relatively simple one. Tables of overs to be deducted for any period of delay were provided and the calculation of the target rate was based on runs per over. The method, however, was too simplistic and usually gave an advantage to the team batting second: and so, from 1997, we have the Duckworth–Lewis tables.

The method of calculating revised targets in rain-affected limited overs matches is almost worth a separate study in its own right. The straightforward, but in many ways, unfair runs per over method was superseded in the 1992 World Cup in Australia by a scheme which took account of the highest scoring overs and the pendulum swung to the other extreme to favouring the team batting first, since if there were more maiden overs in the first innings than overs lost, the team batting second would require the same number of runs, but in fewer overs. The England–South Africa semi-final when South Africa, batting second, left the field requiring 22 from 13 balls and returned after a 12-minute break, requiring 21 from 1, hastened the demise of that particular scheme.

Subsequently, fairer methods were devised based on targets of discounted total runs plus one and used in the Benson and Hedges World Series in Australia and the Wills World Cup in India, Pakistan and Sri Lanka, albeit with different rates of discount. In South Africa, something called the Clarke curve was used.

The latest refinement is the aforementioned Duckworth–Lewis method, devised by Frank Duckworth of the Royal Statistical Society and Tony Lewis of the University of the West of England, Bristol, and based on the principle of adjusting the target by the percentage of the run-scoring resources of the innings, the percentage not only depending on overs lost, but the stage of the innings at which they are lost and the number of wickets that have fallen. The notchers would not have understood all this; it is questionable whether all umpires and scorers do, and fairly certain that the finer detail will remain beyond the grasp of most players and spectators.

The calculations are, however, nowhere near as complicated as some of the less well-informed critics of the system have tried to make out: computer software will do the arithmetic anyway, and in the event of a breakdown, the sums at any rain-break are no more complicated than a simple subtraction and percentage calculation.

There may well be logistical difficulties on some grounds, especially when a break for rain is particularly brief, in communicating the required information to those who need to know – captains, umpires, scoreboard operators, the public address announcer and the Press – but those are not a failing of the method itself.

Certainly, the compilation of the tables from a database of previous matches will be beyond the comprehension of the non-statistician, but just as it is not necessary to understand aerodynamics to bowl or appreciate reverse swing, nor to comprehend the physiology of hand-eye co-ordination to play or admire a cover drive, so it is quite possible to participate in or enjoy the pursuit of a revised target without having the advanced statistical expertise to know how that target is calculated.

There is little doubt that Duckworth–Lewis is capable of further refinement. For instance, at the moment, it takes no account of the enhanced run-scoring opportunities in the first 15 overs of 50-over matches, as an insufficient number have been played under these relatively new regulations which encourage the 'pinch-hitting' approach. One assumes, however, that as the latter becomes a feature of the limited overs game, tables will be revised to take account of it. In the meantime, Duckworth–Lewis, despite one or two minor imperfections, is the fairest method yet invented and my guess is that it will soon be an accepted and integral part of the limited overs game. A brief description of how the method works is included at Appendix B.

Dr George Christos, Lecturer in Applied Mathematics at Curtin University of Technology in Perth, has proposed a scheme which involves a wicket being forfeited for each five overs lost. (7) It has the undoubted advantage of simplicity, but has been rejected on the grounds that it would mean a fundamental change to the nature of the game. So, for the time being at any rate, Duckworth–Lewis rules – it was used in the 1999 World Cup – and domestically is now used by all full ICC members with the exception of Australia and Sri Lanka.

Because of the relative ease with which PA Cricket Record is able to generate a printout – either of a single innings or a complete match – it is relatively straightforward, if perhaps time-consuming at the end of what may have been a match extending well into the final session of the final day, to produce several of them. At Surrey after the final match liaison with the Press, it has been my practice to prepare full match printouts for the opposition scorer, the Librarian and Yearbook Editor, as well as intermediate innings printouts for the Captain, the Manager and the scorecard up-dater.

It is not technologically difficult to press the appropriate button on the printer, but what used to take time were the manual amendments and additions. In 1995, the software was such that there was space for only six bowlers per innings: on those not infrequent occasions when more were used, the statistics for the seventh and subsequent bowlers had to be written in by hand. Fortunately, this deficiency was remedied for the 1996 season when there was provision for eleven bowlers.

In addition to all this, there is a return to the ECB to be completed headed 'Return of Over Rate, Run Rate and Match Result'. It looks more complicated than it is and its completion soon becomes second nature, but it still has to be remembered. For Championship matches, each county provides an independent return; for limited overs matches, there is one return for the match, so there is a signature to give or collect before the visiting scorer can be on his way down the road.

When all this has been done, a hand-written summary of the scores and any significant features is prepared for transmission by fax to the local cable television station. There may be minor variations for other county scorers, but in no case is the work for the match over when the final ball is bowled. In many ways it is only just beginning.

Averages in the traditional form for each of the four competitions are prepared and distributed weekly by PA Cricket Record to the County Office and to the County Scorer's home address. Usually, these are error-free and provide a useful check on one's own arithmetic.

But most coaches and cricket managers require more and on a monthly basis I provide the following:

(a) Scoring rates for limited overs matches in terms of runs per hundred balls;

(b) Analysis of dismissals (including fielding positions where batsmen were caught);

(c) Economy rates in terms of runs conceded per over.

At Surrey, I provide similar information for the 2nd XI; at other clubs the service is provided by the 2nd XI scorer. The nature and extent of it may vary, but the fact remains that it is done and that it provides a valuable information service to the club.

The advent of David Gilbert and an Australian-style management approach at the Foster's Oval in 1996 led to a more scientific approach to cricket and the sensible use of statistical analysis as a management tool. Previous results on grounds where Surrey were scheduled to play were analysed, as were the strengths and weaknesses of the opposition, using the statistics as a major contributory element with the object, as Vinnie Jones , former captain of Wimbledon Football Club, would have it, of taking out their main geezer.

The statistical approach has also been adopted by the ECB's Pitches Research Group whose analyses include for each first-class county runs per wicket and the percentage of wickets taken by spin in the first and second innings and in the third and fourth innings. Armed with this information it should be possible to rival league tables for primary schools by constructing something like a pitch deterioration index which could be one of the factors taken into account by a toss-winning captain in coming to a decision whether to bat or field.

Scorers are thus providing their counties not only with a statistical service, but with an information service that will assist coaching, tactics and indeed selection. 'Cricket Wizard', to which reference is made in the previous chapter will provide more information, but is not as yet widely used outside South Africa.

Information required by county coaches may vary: one – now departed – was particularly keen to know the number of ones, twos, threes, fours and sixes in any particular innings. Quite how he used the information is a mystery to me, but it is all part of a picture illustrating that the County Scorer is not merely passively recording statistical information, but refining and recasting it, so that it is of positive use to his club.

A further responsibility undertaken periodically throughout the season is the checking of information for *Wisden*. Bill Frindall, as the Almanack's chief statistician co-ordinates the whole operation, picking up details from the Press and sending them to the scorers for checking. In theory, as scorers supply the information to the Press through the medium of Cricket Record, it should be the same when it gets back to them: in practice, it often isn't, as misprints, mistakes and gremlins get into the system.

There are times, however, when retrospective adjustments have to be made. It may happen for instance that a four is subsequently deemed to be a six or that the scorers do not know whether a batsman has been given LBW or caught behind the wicket, stumped or run out (It may happen on occasion that the batsman does not know!), so an intelligent guess has to be made for transmission to the Press at the time, perhaps to be amended later, after consultation with the umpires.

For their work for *Wisden* which, in truth, is not terribly time-consuming, scorers receive a small honorarium, plus a complimentary copy of the famous yellow book.

Some scorers are responsible for handling players' meal allowances and are regarded by players as a useful depositary for wallets, watches, jewellery and other valuables and one further duty, verging on the irrelevant to the players, but one of supreme importance to some committee members is the custodianship of the club flag, including its transport to away fixtures, negotiating with the groundstaff for its display on an appropriate flag-pole and retrieving it at the end of the match. As indicated above, there are a number of additional duties to be performed at the end of a match; some scorers travel with the players, who are rarely keen to hang around too long, and it is far from unknown for the flag to be remembered when the scorer is several miles along the motorway. It would perhaps be a sensible solution for each county to issue the other 17 with large stamped addressed envelopes to enable lonely flags to be returned to their appropriate base.

Other duties tend to arise from the very nature of the job, such as scoring at benefit and six-a-side matches, keeping career statistics up to date, providing information for benefit brochures and for sponsors whose players receive so much per run, wicket or catch (All bribes from the sponsored willingly accepted!).

The situation overseas is not quite identical in that scorers do not travel with their State, provincial or island side and the home authority provides both scorers for a match. Presumably visiting officials and/or the Press help with any problems of player identification and there is no suggestion that the scoring is any less professional or any less unbiassed for being home-based, but there must inevitably be less involvement and less of a feeling of being part of the team than is the case in England where team and scorer tend to travel and live together at away matches.

Nor does involvement cease when stumps are drawn for the season: most scorers have some kind of involvement with the *Club Yearbook* which may range from simply checking the proofs to writing the whole thing from scratch. Some scorers also act as their Club Statistician, there is the lunch and Annual General Meeting of the Association of County Cricket Scorers and for those on the Committee and Working Parties more frequent meetings. At all levels, particularly where there is an involvement with the Association of Cricket Umpires and Scorers – an organisation of some 6,500 members operating at all levels of the game – scorers are either training or being trained.

So, one way and another, scorers do tend to do just a little more than record runs and acknowledge signals!

Chapter Six

The Status and Pay of Scorers

Where then do scorers stand in cricket's complex hierarchy and what financial rewards are there for fulfilling the range of obligations described in the last chapter? The answers vary from time to time, from club to club and from scorer to scorer; but it has in general been a little lower than the angels and more often than not, considerably lower.

In her admirable history of umpires and umpiring, Teresa McLean comments on the high status enjoyed by both umpires and scorers in the eighteenth century:

> Scorers at sophisticated games kitted themselves out in smart clothes, moved out of the field of play and sat at tables, watching for umpires' signals and writing the score. Most cricket was pretty rough and so were its notchers, but by 1775 scorers were second only to umpires as status symbols at clubs like the Star and Garter. (1)

This apparently elevated status did not last too long, however, and there is anecdotal evidence that by the mid-nineteenth century, scorers (often pensioned-off umpires) had come to be regarded as the poor relations of the game. Again, Teresa McLean reports that William Caldecourt of Stockton-on-Tees and John Bayley of Mitcham, previously distinguished umpires, were found scoring at Lord's by the Rev. J. Pycroft:

> ...they were sitting on kitchen chairs with a bottle of black ink tied to an old stump to keep it safe, an uncomfortable length of paper on their knees, and large tin telegraph letters above their heads. 'Tis a pity two such men should EVER not be umpires. (2)

W.G. Grace attributes the slow advance of scoring to the educational level of its practioners and, referring to cricket's early days, writes in 1891:

Scorers were not sufficiently educated to enter in writing the runs as they were made, and the primitive form of cutting a notch in a piece of wood was resorted to. A deeper notch was made every tenth run. Rarely were individual innings recorded in other than club matches: and it is difficult to say when the important clubs began to keep complete and reliable results of their matches. (3)

In 1846, the year the first 'telegraph' was installed at Lord's, scorers for MCC, sometimes as we have seen, former umpires, sometimes 'bowlers of the ground' not otherwise engaged, were paid £1 per match, reduced to 10s if the match did not last more than a day. Players and umpires received £2 with the same 50 per cent reduction for a one-day match and there was a £1 win bonus for players for matches of two days or more. (4) The hierarchy of players–umpires–scorers and a rough 3-2-1 payment ratio was thus established. The hierarchy has remained constant, though there have been variations on the payment ratio.

Whatever the status of scorers, however, comments on their competence begin fairly early. As we have seen, the first match for which the 'full' scores have survived was Kent v All England played at the Artillery Ground, London, in 1744. The match was included in the first volume of *Scores and Biographies* and the report includes the following:

The score gives no initials, and does not mention which Newland, which Harris or which Mills obtained wickets; but many matches in this collection (owing to the laziness of the scorers), are incomplete in this respect. (5)

Some would say that this noble tradition of scorers' attitudes and competence has persisted over 250 years!

Indeed, throughout *Scores and Biographies*, Haygarth is severely critical of scorers, viewing them as careless, lazy and inaccurate, a judgement applied equally to scores of matches received from North America and Australasia. The indictment may not be without justification, but one wonders how far Haygarth appreciates that, as indicated in the last chapter, scorers see their primary obligation as providing a service to players, officials and spectators of a particular match at a particular time and the responsibility of providing information for statisticians, the Press and posterity as still important, but rather more peripheral. Certainly there is an element of the tail wagging the dog when he rails against the practice of five-ball overs on the grounds that it upsets his calculations of balls bowled and there is a danger of distorting perspective if we assume the Laws and customs of the game should be revamped for the convenience of statisticians and scorers.

Nevertheless, there is some evidence of the elevation of scorers in the mid-nineteenth century, at least in a literal, if not a metaphorical, sense. Alfred D. Taylor reports that:

> It was about this time [1839] that the scoring 'perch' was erected at Lord's being an elevated platform some eight feet in height, which coign of advantage was gained by mounting a ladder. There was no shelter of any description, but it placed the scorers out of reach of the ever-questioning public and scores came to be more accurately reported in consequence. Prior to its introduction, the scorers occupied a seat on the ground and the incessant enquiries for information sadly distracted the scorers. (6)

A similar construction appeared at Canterbury in 1847:

> ... a stand for the scorers, who were thus out of reach of pestering. (7)

More than a century and a half later, the sentiment will doubtless find an echo in the heart of many a club and village scorer.

Status is only partially separable from pay and it is a truth universally acknowledged that scorers are not the best paid of those associated with first-class cricket and there is no scorer on the county circuit making a living from scoring alone. Like nursing, the motivation lies in the provision of a service, rather than in financial gain. It is still not unknown for scorers to operate on an honorary, expenses-only basis and all need to supplement their very limited earnings from other sources. The general attitude has been to regard scoring as a paid hobby and to take the view that because scorers enjoy the job, because financial gain is not their main motivation, and because if all county scorers were to resign tomorrow, 36 more could easily be recruited, there is no need to pay them much more than a pittance plus expenses. Nevertheless, the range of computing, statistical and interpretational skills now associated with the job compared with even five years ago make such a view increasingly difficult to maintain.

There have, however, been times in the past when scorers' pay has compared with that of umpires and almost with that of the players, but sponsorship, prize money and the establishment of the Professional Cricketers' Association have been instrumental in widening the gap. By comparison, the scorers' equivalent, the Association of County Cricket Scorers is still at the nappy stage.

Evidence from the minutes of Kent County Cricket Club suggest that there was a time when scorers' pay was not too far behind that of the players and compared very well with wages elsewhere in the economy. Cricketers today are paid less than most professional sportsmen and their career span is short.

At the turn of the century, their actual rates of pay were generous compared with skilled and semi-skilled workers. In the main, however, it was summer employment only and it was a short career. Scorers could at least expect to go on longer and at Kent were reasonably well paid.

The Kent minutes record a rate of 5s per day in 1875. By 1880, however, the rates varied from £2 to £4 10s per match depending on the venue. No expenses were paid and professionals, umpires and scorers were expected to meet their own travelling and accommodation costs. Professionals were paid £5 per match which was increased at the 1880 AGM to £6 for matches more than 200 miles from Maidstone.

By 1900, scorers pay rates had stabilised to £4 for home matches and £5 for away matches at venues such as Manchester and Dewsbury. It is a reflection of a different social era and relative importance of fixtures that the Oxford University fixture at Maidstone attracted an additional £1. In an age of limited inflation, the pay of the professionals had remained at the same rate over 20 years. The balance has changed over the years as the Cricketers' Association has become more powerful, the influence of Kerry Packer felt and money poured into the game, so that in broad terms, a county scorer is paid about a third the rate of a capped professional.

The accounts of the Canterbury Festival for the late nineteenth century indicate that beer was about a shilling a gallon. So, a scorer's pay for a home match would buy about 80 gallons. To buy the same quantity today, should he feel the urge to do so, a scorer – or any one else for that matter – would require well over £1,000. They are paid less than that for Test matches, considerably less for other first-class matches. Rates of pay have not kept pace and it is not possible for the county scorer today to keep himself in the style to which he would wish to be accustomed on his county pay alone, such pay being usually regarded as pocket money to be supplemented by one or more of a pension, a winter job, perhaps as club statistician or yearbook editor, or income from business or self-employment.

At the turn of the century, however, it was quite possible to live on £4 per week, as the following rates of pay and prices taken from the Kent accounts indicate:

Professionals £5 per match
Umpires £5 per match
Bowlers 50s per week
2nd XI Scorer £1 10s per match
Telegraph attendants £1 10s per match
Secretary £20 per annum.

In Canterbury week 1876, nine men on the ground and telegraph were paid £9 between them.

Subscriptions were a guinea which permitted entrance to the ground for a member, his carriage, three occupants and coachman. (8)

Outside the cricket world, the following weekly rates of pay between 1906 and 1913 are interesting and useful comparators:

Foremen £2 4s
Coalface workers £2 2s
Fitters £1 15s
London bus driver £2
Agricultural labourers 19s
Women typists £1 11s (9)

Certainly it appears that at least in Kent at the beginning of the century it was possible to earn something of a living as a scorer in a way that was not possible everywhere at the time and certainly has not been possible in most places since.

It may well be that Kent were unusually generous in their approach to scorers' pay. By contrast, in 1905, Bill Ferguson was paid £2 per week (later increased to £3) for his scoring and baggage master duties for the Australian touring side: his train fares were met, though he travelled third class and the rest of the party first but his travel to and from England was at his own expense, accounting for £34 of his total tour earnings. (10) Whatever motivated 'Fergie' to abandon his steady job as a filing clerk for a Sydney Directory, it was certainly not the prospect of making a quick buck.

The status of the job was consonant with the pay; in addition to travelling separately from the team, he soon became aware of the sharp class distinctions in English society (at that time also reflected in Australian society to a greater extent than they are today), he was required to eat with the local professionals rather than with the team and to make his own accommodation arrangements. His welcome at Lord's for the Gentlemen of England v Australians match was not the most cordial:

The venue was Lord's, the headquarters of the game of cricket, the Mecca of everyone connected with it. I felt quite proud as I climbed the stairs leading to the score box... Deflation arrived swiftly on entering the cubicle allotted to the scorers. Two gentlemen, poring over the largest scoring books I had ever seen were in full possession of the available space. I introduced myself as the Australian scorer, but after looking me up and down one of them dismissed me thus, 'We don't require any more scorers. There's no room for you in here.' (11)

Fergie was never allowed to wear the tie of the Australian touring team and his 50 years' service to what was then the Imperial Cricket Conference were rewarded by a whip-round which realised £250 and a further cheque for £200 from the Australian Cricket Board. No testimonial, no benefit, no pension. (12)

Matters have improved. Travel and accommodation arrangements for overseas tours are now identical to those of the players and although the fee is 'modest' (ECB's description, not mine!) all expenses are met, a uniform is provided and socially at any rate the scorer is regarded as part of the team, though the particulars for the 1994 England tour to the West Indies did include a requirement for an ability to 'melt into the background'. However, of the Test-playing countries, only England, Australia and New Zealand are accompanied by a scorer; the remainder arrange to have one (or more) appointed by the host nation. And no 'A' team has yet taken a scorer on tour.

A report in *The Daily Telegraph* on 9 December 1996 on the South Australia v England 'A' match referred to the scorers' confusing White and Butcher and the spectators being uncertain as to when Butcher reached his 50. In fairness, the confusion was probably the scoreboard operators' rather than the scorers', but an England scorer might just have been able to point out that Butcher was the left-hander!

But back to the domestic scene. Scorers have already been referred to as the poor relations of the game and we have seen Teresa McLean's description of their lowly status in the nineteenth century compared to the eighteenth. On balance, matters had not improved by the beginning of the twentieth when their place in the hierarchy is perhaps epitomised by a minute of the Ground Committee of Surrey County Cricket Club which records expenditure of £1 2s 6d on the Scorers Room and £6 10s on the stables. (13)

Certainly, Surrey appear to have been less generous to their scorers than Kent and there is a larger differential between players' and scorers' pay than on the other side of the Medway. The General Meeting of 1853 approved a proposal that 'bowlers of the ground' required to act as scorers in one-day matches be paid 15s per day. Those playing were paid £3 for losing, £4 for winning plus second-class travelling expenses.

The gap in social standing between gentlemen and players was clear cut and has been well documented and, certainly in terms of pay, the gap between players and scorers was large. For the best players in the mid-Victorian era £5 per match was the norm (14) and from this they were, in general, responsible for their own travel, accommodation and other expenses.

Surrey are generally regarded as having taken a more benevolent attitude than many towards their professionals, but Julius Caesar ended his life in poverty and was found dead at the Railway Tavern in Godalming. Only three former Surrey professionals came to bury Caesar. For Edward Pooley, one of the best wicket-keepers of his generation, the choice was the workhouse or the river. (15)

Scorers at least had the advantage of having longer careers, but their treatment by the committee was one of occasionally benevolent despotism. Pooley had been engaged as scorer for three matches in 1881, having also found some work in a billiard saloon in 1880. For the 1882 season, a Mr Creed was appointed, an allowance of 5s per day being made to him for club matches round London. Towards the end of the season, however, he had the temerity to approach the committee with a suggestion that he be paid for the third day of matches scheduled for three days but finishing in two. Wielding a sharp two-edged sword, the committee records in its minutes for the meeting held on 5 September:

> It was resolved that Mr Creed be paid 10s for the third day of matches completed in two days and that a note be sent to him dispensing with his services from this date.

Until this time, scoring appointments had been spasmodic and usually from the ground staff who were not playing. There are regular references throughout the 1852 minutes to one Taylor doing the scoring, but the first long term appointment comes with Fred Boyington who held the office from 1884 to his death in 1927.

The club's treatment of him is perhaps best described as chequered, though it must be recalled that we are talking of a time which pre-dated organised labour, trade unionism and the protective employment legislation that characterises the employer–employee relationship a century later. Surrey, however, were perhaps among the more enlightened employers of the time and were in the vanguard of introducing winter pay for their players in 1894. (16)

It is clear from the minutes, however, that the scorer had a permanent struggle to make ends meet. From 1898, he received a loan of £10 to tide him over the winter, to be repaid by the following June: a request for £15 in 1903 was refused; in 1905, however, a loan of £25 was agreed and it became the practice for Boyington to receive an annual advance of £25 and to pay it back in two instalments the following June and August.

In 1913, a request from Boyington, now with almost 30 years' service to Surrey, that he be allowed to score in club matches when no county match was taking place was, in the bland prose of the minutes, 'not entertained'.

The winter loan arrangement came unstuck in the 1915 season when the First World War caused all first-class cricket to be cancelled and Boyington was unable to repay the loan. A grant of 5s per week was made to him until the end of 1915: a request for it to be continued until the resumption of county cricket met with a negative response. An application for a further loan in 1916 was declined. County cricket resumed in 1919 and in November 1920 the committee was writing to Boyington asking for the repayment of the £25 advanced six years earlier.

In the 1920s, a benefit was granted to him to which the committee contributed £25, but declined a request for a second collection during the Yorkshire match. The next minute records a contribution of 250 guineas to a special fund to mark Jack Hobbs's achievement of 126 first-class centuries. No one would argue that a scorer's contribution to cricket is in the same category as that of a world-class batsman, but the contrast in treatment is stark.

In 1927, after the death of Boyington, the committee agreed to continue his £1 per week pension to his widow for the remainder of her life. There are longer records of service than his 42 years, however; George Austin of Warwickshire had a career extending from 1911 to 1963 and Leo Bullimore scored for 51 years for Northamptonshire.

Boyington was followed by Herbert Strudwick who appended to a 30-year playing career a similar period as scorer before his final retirement in 1958 when he was followed by Andrew Sandham. Both were part of a tradition prevalent in a number of counties whereby the scorer's job was offered to a former professional cricketer. The custom is one which has all but died with better pay and better remunerated post-retirement employment. Of the eighteen first-class counties only Middlesex now rigidly adhere to the tradition: in 1946 seven of the seventeen scorers (17) were or had been contracted to their county as professional cricketers; by 1993, with the retirement of Ted Lester, it was down to one, Harry Sharp at Middlesex being replaced by Mike Smith.

The Hampshire Accounts books (18) for 1922 reveal that the scorer, Len Sprankling, then in the second of his 32 seasons with the club, received varying amounts, usually more for away matches to include an expenses element, but at somewhere round about £3 per match it is roughly between one-third and one-fifth of the pay of the players.

When Herbert Strudwick was appointed Surrey scorer in 1927, he was paid £4 per week (19); capped players between the wars had a guaranteed year-round minimum of £400. (20) There were various bits and pieces for appearing, winning and overnight expenses, but the scorer's overall pay would be less than 50 per cent of that of the capped players, which of course he himself had been and was in all likelihood treated more generously because of his 30 years' service to the club than a newcomer might have been.

The remuneration of scorers as recorded in *Wisden* between 1914 and 1973 makes an interesting sociological commentary as well as throwing light on the importance of Australian tours, compared with those of other Test-playing countries. The Board of Control for Home Test Matches, established by MCC in 1898 and the Test and County Cricket Board into which it was absorbed in 1968, determined annually a fee for scorers in Test matches. In 1914 it was £5 per match (Professional players at the time were paid £20); in 1922 it was £7 10s, dropping to £5 for 1931 to 1933 and 1935 to 1937 and being restored to £7 10s in 1939. In the 'Australian' years of 1930, 1934 and 1938, it rose to a princely £10.

Post-war, it was £15 in 1947, £20 in 1948 (Australia again!), dropping back to £10 for 1949 and reverting to £20 the following year. It then went up to £25 in 1957 and remained at that level for almost a decade and a half when it was adjusted upwards to £30 in 1971. Over the same period, during which the retail price index rose by something over 50 per cent, players' pay rose from £100 to £150 per match and umpires' pay from £65 to £100 per match.

These were of course pre-Packer days when cricketers were poor relations among sportsmen and even now, they are in a similar relative position to footballers, golfers and tennis players. Scorers then were and remain the poor relations of the poor relations.

Already in 1865, *Wisden* was in some cases beginning to record the identity of umpires in its match scorecards. Scorers, apart from an acknowledgement in small print for their assistance in checking scorecards, do not appear until 1994 and then only with their club officials, not under each match.

It would be gratifying to report that by 1997, the introduction of laptop computers and the Duckworth–Lewis method had acted as catalysts to improve the pay and status and that the cricketing establishment had begun to recognise the professionalism now required of scorers and to treat them with a little more respect and sensitivity. It would also be quite misleading.

The main cause of polarisation between county scorers and the ECB in 1997 lay in the appointment of Malcolm Ashton for a third consecutive winter tour and details of the genesis and evolution of that dispute are contained in Chapter Twelve. There were rumblings of disharmony before that, however, with overt statements by Ted Lester, Chairman of ACCS which would, had he been contracted to the ECB or a county, have resulted in his being charged with bringing the game into disrepute. There was no answer, nor could there be, to Ted's rejoinder that he was contracted to no one and that he could say what he liked.

The cause? Medallions issued to players and umpires but not to scorers. With a direct swipe at Cornhill Insurance and Benson and Hedges, Ted wrote in an open letter:

> I have to say that it is a continuing affront to the status of scorers that they are continually overlooked by certain sponsors who fail to appreciate that umpires and scorers work together as a team and are doing the scorers a disservice by recognising only one half of the team.

He goes on to castigate both Benson and Hedges, whose Special Events Director expressed an unwillingness to change his Company's policy on the number of medallions presented, and Cornhill who responded negatively to a request by TCCB in 1996 that medallions be made available for England scorers. His comments received considerable support in *The Scorer* (they would, wouldn't they?), but there was only a slight softening of attitude on the part of the sponsors.

B & H have had their policy changed for them anyway by the Government's decision that sponsorship of sports events by tobacco companies be discontinued, but in the meantime agreed to make available three additional medallions in addition to the thirteen awarded to each of the two teams in the finals and the Cricket Operations Manager of the ECB wrote to each county suggesting that scorers might be considered for one of the extra medallions. Cornhill agreed that scorers might be presented with a framed certificate.

As chance would have it, in 1997 I scored the Benson and Hedges Final at Lord's and the Sixth Test Match at the Foster's Oval. Surrey used 14 players in the competition and a Twelfth Man at Lord's who was not one of the 14 – $(13 + 3) - (14 + 1) = 1$. I received no medallion. By contrast, John Holder, the TV Replay Umpire for the Benson and Hedges Final who was not called on to make a decision all day, is highly amused, proud and delighted to be the holder of a medal he did nothing at all to earn. A certificate for the Test Match would normally have been presented on the fifth day: the preparation of the Oval pitch ensured there was no fifth day and my certificate sat in the ECB offices at Lord's all winter before being 'presented' to me at a pre-season scorers' seminar some seven months after the event it commemorated.

The physical absence of medallions and the delay in the physical emergence of certificates concern me not a jot. Like the host in the eucharist, they are the outward and visible sign of an inward and invisible grace – a grace which has remained totally invisible in the case of the ECB, sponsors and counties who appear rock-solid in their corporate determination to keep scorers in their place at the bottom of the heap.

The ECB took a similar hard line on the question of scorers' pay for the Benson and Hedges Final. Until 1995, the section of the Rules relating to the Final listed under payments to be made by the ground authority on behalf of the Board out of match receipts:

Scorers' remuneration, travelling and accommodation expenses – as for Texaco Trophy (Rule 4 (iv) (b) (i)).

This did not appear in the 1996 and 1997 Rules and I wondered what the reasons behind its omission might be. The kindest interpretation was that it was an oversight, although this appeared unlikely as the other items on the list remained and had been renumbered (i) to (iv), rather than (ii) to (v). The alternative conclusion was that it had been deliberately removed and if this were correct, it seemed that we had yet another example of scorers being kicked in their few remaining teeth.

It could, I suppose, be argued that as scorers were being paid by their clubs, there was no justification for further payment and while there was some merit in that, the counter-argument would be that most scorers were paid an annual salary or fee by their club and the two engaged in the B & H Final were working when their sixteen colleagues had a day off.

I approached the ECB with these thoughts and received a reply from the Finance Director that the regulations were amended several years ago to remove the anomaly of a fee being charged against the match accounts in respect of scoring services provided by MCC. If for 'several' one reads 'two', that statement is doubtless factually correct. It used to be the case that for the major matches at Lord's the MCC provided a scorer or scorers in addition to the scorers of the participating clubs – Oxford, Cambridge, the participating Cup Finalists or whoever. For a couple of years, in 1993 and 1994, I was one of those scorers, sharing duties with Eddie Solomon who kept the book while I operated the computer and received the 'as for Texaco Trophy' remuneration. However, as the computer software has become more reliable and scorers happier with it, a decision has been taken or perhaps emerged by osmosis, that the laptop will be operated by the scorers of the participating finalists.

That arrangement is absolutely pragamtic and sensible. In any event the cramped scoring conditions and minimal amount of space left in the temporary scorebox in the Warner Stand, following its invasion by South African technicians trying to get to grips with the idiosyncracies of the new scoreboard (see Chapter Eight), have left precious little space for additional scorers. Shades of Fergie's first visit to Lord's. Now it is the MCC scorers who have been deposed. However, notwithstanding the reshuffling and irrespective of changing financial arrangements between ECB and MCC, it remains the case that Jack Foley, the Kent scorer, and I provided a service on behalf of the game's Governing Body and the ground authority which in 1995 was paid for and in 1997 was not.

For my final example of the way in which scorers have been treated with cavalier arrogance, I return to The Oval where the ghosts of Creed and Boyington and the committees which employed them still haunt the corridors, though this time the differences are not about finances, but working conditions and the invasion of The Oval scorebox by the paraphernalia and razzmatazz surrounding Sunday League cricket. The relationships between cricket and the marketing of it and between sport and business, are complex ones which have been covered elsewhere – especially by Graeme Wright in his admirable *Betrayal, The Struggle for Cricket's Soul* – and normally has but a peripheral impact on the scoring operation. In 1997, however, on Sundays at The Oval, that struggle became over-intrusive. Surrey is not alone in attempting to attract a larger and different clientele to Sunday cricket by the introduction of marketing gimmicks such as kiddies' games, quizzes with cash prizes, grown men dressed as wild animals, pop music accompanying players to the wicket and a big-top style of presentation. Members can either resign or not attend: players, umpires, office staff and scorers can either find another job – or, more realistically, just put up with it.

However, the decision to make the scorebox the nerve-centre of the operation was one of which I was made aware only as it was being implemented on the first Sunday of the season and the normal dedicated workspace being hi-jacked by electricians and PA men. Consultation on the compatibility of this kind of activity with the scoring operation was clearly not an issue about which the club's decision-makers felt obliged to contact its scorer or its Match Manager and representations to have the scoring and PA functions separated have met with a negative response. It appears that there is nowhere else on a Test match ground from which the PA could operate. It does during Test matches, but that, I am told, is a 'different level of service' – whatever that may mean.

Scoring a 40-over match can be a somewhat pressurised operation in itself, the more so when scorers have to keep a weather eye on the possibility of 'doing a Duckworth–Lewis' and becomes more so alongside what Michael Henderson described in *The Times* as 'the almost constant noise from the public address system that rings in the ears when you leave The Oval on Sundays whether it is Johnny Gold's [sic] rallying cries or the tinny tunes.' (21)

The advantages of having the scorers adjacent to the PA are referred to in the previous chapter, but these were considerably outweighed by the disadvantages. There are two occasions when scorers need especially to consult with each other, namely, the fall of a wicket and the end of an over, and these were precisely the occasions which coincided with high-decibel pop music or radiophone contact with the organisers of the free beer, tea-time target competitions etc. Whatever the pros and cons of subordinating scoring to salesmanship, to subject visiting scorers to such working conditions is at best inconsiderate, at worst ill-mannered and almost certainly in contravention of the Health and Safety at Work Act.

Consultation with umpires about overs lost to the weather, Duckworth–Lewis calculations etc. also requires the kind of fairly quiet working environment which was absent on summer Sundays in 1997. There was one occasion when the background noise in the box caused the scorers to misinterpret a call of one short from the square leg umpire as a call for a no ball and, following a tea-time consultation, Yorkshire, who believed they had brought up the 200 with a six from the last ball of the innings, found their total dragged back to 198. As it happened, the mistake occurred late in the first innings and was corrected at tea-time. Had it been in the second innings, it might have affected the result of the match and there would have been egg on a number of faces. There is little doubt, however, where the blame for getting the score wrong would be perceived to be.

I have been reminded of my alleged obligation to support a corporate policy to which I have not contributed or even been invited to contribute – at least questionable in days of worker participation when Huxley, Kafka and Orwell are no longer seen as the standard for industrial relations at the end of the second millennium. Now the scorebox is not mine but provided to enable me to do a job and those appointed by the committee to manage the club can use it for any legal purpose. That much is not in question. But most workers, whether in factories, offices, shops or railway premises, might bristle at least slightly if they found their workplace invaded by those with little connection with their own. But scorers are expected to passively acquiesce and in so doing confirm their position at the bottom of the hierarchical heap.

In fairness, it should be mentioned that in 1998 the razzmatazz element in the AXA League was scaled down, though the change to a lower-key approach was probably more to do with public response, fewer Sunday afternoon matches and the fact that Surrey spent the whole season anchored at the foot of the table and were the first county to qualify for Division 2 of the new National League. My suspicions that the welfare of the scorers was not a major motivating factor in the apparent change of policy were confirmed when for the day–night matches played at the Foster's Oval, the one floodlight pylon which needed to be adjacent to the playing area rather than outside the public seating was strategically placed directly in front of the scorebox thereby obscuring a large part of the playing area. That, however, was luxury compared with the situation at Headingley for the 'Roses' match when the problem of floodlights reflecting from the glass-fronted press box into the players' eyes was solved by the installation of a large blackout curtain. Press and scorers thought that the total eclipse scheduled for the following year had come early.

The treatment of scorers for the 1999 World Cup was absolutely consistent with that throughout the century in that they are being asked to operate on an 'expenses only' basis. It is scarcely surprising therefore that of the twelve appointed (one for each competing team, plus two reserves, with Australia and Scotland providing their own), only three were County 1st XI scorers. Doubtless the residue of 2nd XI scorers, scoreboard and computer operators did a thorough, professional job, but there is an awful lot of experience that is not being used and one would have thought that the ECB would have been anxious to avoid a repetition of events in the 1996 World Cup in India and Pakistan when Bill Frindall was able to write:

> In the early days, many of these internationals were scored on loose sheets or in reserve scorebooks and the original records have gone astray or been destroyed. In numerous cases, the two official records do not agree and contain obvious errors. Often specialist scorers are not available and players or occasional amateurs are drafted in. Even such a recent and high-profile tournament as the 1996 World Cup produced a host of scoring errors and differences. (22)

The ECB and Event Manager took the view that pay was not the main motivation for scorers applying for and accepting the appointments. That assumption was almost certainly correct. It would, I am sure, be equally correct when applied to players, umpires and match officials, but I am not aware that any of them had been asked to operate on an expenses-only basis.

The World Cup was a massive commercial bonanza with a predicted turnover of some £40 million; to pay scorers the usual rate applicable to Limited Overs Internationals and provide the usual package of complimentary tickets and hospitality for a couple of guests would have cost a miniscule percentage of that.

The Working Time Regulations effective from 1 October 1998, the National Minimum Wage from 1 April 1999 and their implications for paid holidays and pension rights can work only to the advantage of scorers, but what an indictment on counties as employers that such an external stimulus should be required to improve the employment conditions of some of their most loyal servants.

Chapter Seven

Scoring
for the Media

Newspapers have always found good copy in cricket and, although not a primary source, can often be more informative about events than the actual scorebook. Until about the middle of the nineteenth century, they were the principal means of conveying information about the game to the general public. Then, in 1838, Samuel Morse demonstrated his telegraph to the Franklin Institute – not the total-wickets-last man telegraph that would appear at Lord's a few years later, but an electrical device capable of transmitting information instantly over a distance. Cricket was not slow to realise its potential:

> Oh! 'tis enough to make the Hambledon heroes sit upright in their graves, with astonishment, to think that in the Gentlemen and Players match in 1850, the cricketers of old Sparks' Ground in Edinburgh could actually know the score of the first innings in London before the second had commenced! (1)

Cricket broadcasting had begun, though it was 1927 before the medium of the spoken word was used. Televised cricket was pioneered in 1938; after the war the refinement of a media scorer was added to broadcasting teams and the practice was well established by the time I made my debut for the BBC in February 1994.

"Up the stairs and follow the wires, man," was the concise reply to my enquiry on the whereabouts of the BBC commentary point. I followed the instructions carefully, narrowly avoiding the unanalysed contents of a bucket which descended from somewhere above round about the half-way point, and eventually came upon a large wooden box which, when a few nails had been removed to enable the hinged flaps at the front to be lifted, would, I was reliably informed, make a commentary position unrivalled throughout the Caribbean.

The place was Kensington Oval, Bridgetown, Barbados; the time mid-morning on the eve of the first of five One Day Internationals between

England and West Indies which, along with the series of five Test Matches, would occupy most of my waking hours for the next ten weeks or so. Bill Frindall, the regular scorer, was unable to make the trip and I had offered my services as scorer to the BBC's *Test Match Special* commentary team. The time between the announcement of the appointment and the assumption of duty had passed alarmingly quickly and here I was, whisked from the frozen depths of an English winter and on the verge of what was to prove to be a fairly intense tour of duty in the tropics.

Peter Baxter, the Producer of Test Match Special, arrived and introduced me to Jonathan Agnew the BBC's Cricket Correspondent who formally welcomed me to the World of Cricket Broadcasting. Minutes later Jennifer Sharrier from Cable and Wireless came into the box and started talking of codex, analogue, digital, 54 and 64. It took me only moments to realise, my physics having fallen short of 'O' level some four decades ago, that the technical world of cricket broadcasting was one to which my contribution was going to be precisely nil and that such limited talent as I had would be confined to the scoresheet.

Unlike that of Sky Sports, whose team is accompanied around the Caribbean by two plane loads of complicated gear, the BBC's overseas operation is very much of the shoe-string variety. The complete set of broadcasting equipment is compressed into an economy-size tin box with a handle, and Peter Baxter proved to be a remarkable one-man trinity of producer, technician and commentator.

Scoring for the media is not very different from being the official scorer and there is little difficulty in switching from one to the other without too much of a culture shock. The disquiet of the Association of County Cricket Scorers at the appointment of BBC Television scorer Malcolm Ashton as England scorer for overseas tours arose from unhappiness that one of their number was not chosen, and was not a reflection of the man's competence or his ability to do the job.

There are some differences, however, between being a media scorer and an official scorer, the most immediately striking of which is that one is entirely on one's own. It is of course true that for most of the time a commentary is going alongside. Commentators are very familiar with the players and it is sometimes helpful to rely on their knowledge rather than straining through field-glasses to identify a catcher who has disappeared from view, surrounded by the slip cordon, the wicket-keeper and short legs. But from the point of view of liaison with a fellow scorer and the umpires the position is very much a solo one.

As an official scorer one invariably works at first-class level with the opposition's scorer, so if, like the good Homer, one nods momentarily, there is always a colleague to draw one's attention to the missed wide or leg bye. I am fully aware that clubs below first-class and minor counties level frequently do not provide scorers and the club scorer will often find himself working solo and perhaps operating the scoreboard as well. I make no pretence that this is any less onerous than working for the media, but the main difference is that the solo club scorer has a liaison with the umpire not enjoyed by the media scorer.

The experience drove home the point that what is absolutely crucial in scoring at any level and in any circumstances is to watch and concentrate on every ball and wait for any signal. This latter part is even more important for those not scoring officially where there is not the same direct link with the umpire, and the fact that the unofficial or media scorer may have missed a signal does not concern the men in white coats – nor should it.

Errors of arithmetic can always be corrected later; but there is only the one chance to see and record and once that is missed, it has gone for ever – unless, one has the luxury of television replays, a benefit far from ubiquitous in the world of media scoring.

The most difficult times were those when no commentary was actually taking place. Balmy afternoons in the Caribbean coincide with foggy and frosty evenings in Europe; and there are times when the BBC's programme scheduling causes cricket to take second place to a European football match, a shipping forecast, or *The Archers*. It is at such times that the BBC commentary team go off to relax and leave the scorer in splendid isolation to record the details required for close of play summaries. I particularly recall the tedium of the latter stages of the One Day International in St Vincent. West Indies had amassed 313–6, England had lost wickets early, the result was a foregone conclusion from about the 20-over point, players, spectators and commentary teams had long lost interest and the poor old BBC scorer was left alone to record the proceedings.

A second difference between scoring for the media and being an official scorer is the greater immediacy in that, for example, bowling figures are required as soon as an over has finished. Working with a colleague, there is a traditional ritual of checking the runs scored from the over just finished, the cumulative runs conceded by that bowler and the score at the end of the over. So the check runs something like 'Three off; 33; four on; 76; 1-4-2-8 15' which is scorers' shorthand for 'Three against the bowler, Walsh now has two for 33, four to be added to the total, making 76 of which fifteen are extras, comprising one bye, four leg byes, two wides and eight no balls'. Commentators in general, however, and Jonathan Agnew in particular, like to give the bowling figures as soon as the over is finished.

Consequently, priorities have to be rejigged slightly and I soon developed a technique of having the pencil poised over the bowling analysis sheet as soon as the sixth ball was delivered and entering the analysis as soon as it became clear. I then went back to the worksheet to record the last ball of the over and update the total, extras, each batsman's score and balls faced. Some commentators are excellent at doing mental arithmetic at the same time as giving the commentary, but, as the commentary itself requires a measure of concentration, most understandably are not and I regarded it as part of the scorer's job to have the margin of defeat, the interval lead or runs required to save the follow on immediately available, especially if we were just about to go off air.

Finally, the media scorer is required to produce background statistics to an extent greater than that required from the official scorers. Most county scorers will have with them the personal and career details of their players and details of their team's past performances, but may not always be required to produce them immediately. In general, however, radio and television commentators like to be able to announce that that is Stewart's sixth Test century, his second against the West Indies, it contained twelve fours, came off 272 balls and it is the first time against the West Indies and the eighth time in all that an England batsman has scored a century in each innings of a Test match. To provide such information requires some background research, some anticipation and, I suppose, a measure of luck.

Cable and Wireless, the series sponsors, had provided some background statistics on the tour and I supplemented these by a DIY file of results in previous England–West Indies Test and One Day encounters, along with the individual records of the England touring party and those likely to be selected to represent West Indies. Each of these took up an A4 sheet, the other side of which I used to keep a record of performances on tour. All these were to hand in a ring binder along with the results in the recently concluded Red Stripe Cup, the Playing Regulations for the series and a sheet which I entitled 'Milestones in Sight' on which I listed items such as:

One Day Internationals –
Haynes needs 83 runs for 1000 v England
Lewis needs 2 wickets for 50

Test Matches –
Atherton needs 73 runs for 2000
Lara needs 170 for 1000

As the milestones were approached the figures were amended and a marginal note made of when and where they were passed. In the case of that last statistic, it was of course left way behind and new records established, hardly foreseen when the series began!

Some anticipation certainly helps, as does a handy *Playfair* and *Wisden* and, if a batsmen is 85 not out overnight or at an interval, it would clearly be unprofessional not to have available details of his previous centuries in all Tests and against these particular opponents to be passed to the commentators along with the statistics for the innings immediately the century is reached. If he then gets out in the 90s, the post-it slip (my usual method of passing information to the commentators – much more practical than trying to get behind the microphone) goes in the bin to join its many predecessors, some used by the commentators, others ignored. I considered it better to overprovide rather than underprovide as I believe it better to supply the team with information they do not use, rather than be scrabbling around for it with half an eye on *Wisden*, half an eye on *Playfair*, half an eye on the statistics file and half an eye on the play just in case a single happens to be scored.

One can of course be caught out by the unusual, and, ironically, the most challenging period for the scorer/statistician is not when everything is happening on the field of play, as on those occasions, there is plenty to talk about and the commentators do not require the same amount of 'feed'. It is during the longueurs, or indeed, the breaks for rain or bad light when the commentary tends to wander into other areas and one can be caught out by the obscure or unexpected question. On one such occasion, no balls were under discussion along with the merits and demerits of the current TCCB regulation which provides that in domestic first-class and One Day cricket no balls count two in addition to any runs scored from them.

I happened to know that the first 'eight' (a six scored from a no ball) had been by Peter Such from Joey Benjamin's bowling at the Foster's Oval. As Peter Such had been a former colleague of the BBC's cricket correspondent and not normally noted for his batting prowess, the information provided Jonathan Agnew with a few one liners such as that to Viv Richards: 'Tell me, Viv, what is it that Peter Such has achieved as a batsman that neither you nor Brian Lara have?'

I was lucky. It was just one of those pieces of information stored in the debris of one's sub-conscious internal filing system. Events can, however, take one completely by surprise. I was not present when Dominic Cork took a hat-trick against the West Indies on the fourth morning of the Old Trafford Test in 1995. I did watch it later on the Sky highlights and was intrigued that no one on the Sky commentary team was aware the the last Test Match hat-trick for England was by Peter Loader against West Indies at Headingley in 1957. For some time, they were giving the date as 1959. Just one of those things one is lucky enough to know or unlucky enough not to know.

I believe it was Arnold Palmer who commented how strange it was that the more he practised, the luckier he seemed to be and I suppose it is the same with *Test Match Special* scorers, that the more research they do and the more knowledge they acquire, the luckier they seem to be when questions are fired at them. I do not begin to compare with Bill Frindall and the masses of information which he, as chief statistician to *Wisden* and regular scorer to the BBC, has at his finger tips, nor with BBC Television and Sky Sports and their computerised databases, but my comparatively amateurish Stone Age methods seemed generally to keep the commentators happy.

Scoring for the media does, however, confirm the trends that we observed earlier, namely that in the provision of detail and setting the match in a historical and statistical context, media scoring is ahead of official scoring, the latter having the more limited objective of recording the score for the match in question with only occasional forays into other statistics for the benefit of the ground public address system. From the time of Pratt's scorecards, however, through the time of Lillywhite's printing press and the time of detailed newspaper reports of the nineteenth and early twentieth centuries, through to the time of Sky Sports comprehensive databases which update batting and bowling averages even as runs are scored and conceded, media scoring has been always more detailed, more wide-ranging and often more accurate than the official version.

So much for radio. Scoring for television is not vastly different: Jo King, who scored for Sky Sports on that Caribbean tour and who now does some work for the BBC in overseas matches, uses the same Frindall-type scoresheets for both radio and television. Perhaps the main difference in television scoring was that there was support from the visual graphics team who provided scorecards and a range of statistics, including balls received, bowling analysis, times and balls for fifties and hundreds and details of partnerships.

My own experience of scoring for television is limited to one extraordinary day, though it would be severely misleading to claim it was anything other than absolutely atypical. The occasion was the Autumn equinox 1994 and the end-of-season international six-a-sides at the Foster's Oval organized (I use the participle loosely) by Roland Butcher's 'Cricket Legends'. The format was the one used in the successful Hong Kong six-a-sides and if one sees Test Matches as akin to classical drama and One Day Internationals akin to pantomime, then on the same scale, six-a-side cricket is custard pie farce. Not that there is anything wrong with a modest proportion of custard pie, but a surfeit of the stuff becomes rapidly indigestible. It had been assumed that several thousand would pack the ground to witness this floodlit extravaganza. But the culture of south London and the late evening, late September weather are somewhat different to what pertains in Hong Kong.

I was one of rather too many scorers which one of the many administrative cock-ups which characterised the occasion had produced. It was not an insoluble problem. Being the only one with media scoring experience, I took myself off to score for TV Asia who had no scorer and were covering the tournament live on their local channel as well as beaming it to India and Pakistan and anywhere else in Asia where anyone was interested.

My illusions that scoring for TV Asia would be similar to scoring for the BBC were rudely and abruptly shattered and I found myself not as I had anticipated, alongside the commentators but between two graphics technicians on a shelf halfway back in the Oval Media Centre. As people they were very pleasant, as graphics technicians I am sure they were perfectly competent, but the first question 'What is an over?' indicated their level in the league table of connoisseurship of cricket and made me realise I could be in for a difficult few hours. Matters were compounded as night fell, the less than perfect floodlighting combining with less than clean windows to restrict visibility, make player identification difficult and render the scoreboard completely invisible.

Next day, the six-a-side tournament suffered the same fate as John Cleese's parrot. It was an ex-tournament. It was no more. The players had drawn the absolutely correct conclusion that there was no money to pay them and had withdrawn their services. If there was no money to pay the players, it was an axiomatic and incontrovertible consequence that there would be no resources with which to recompense the scorers and so it turned out. Geoffrey Boycott, who had doubled as expert summariser and match referee, had the good sense to claim and collect his fee up front. The remainder of us were not as worldly wise.

In a hastily prepared press release, Surrey County Cricket Club, while disclaiming any responsibility for the fiasco on the not unreasonable grounds that its role was limited to providing the venue for the event, agreed to reimburse those few members of the general public optimistic enough to have purchased tickets in advance and in addition to provide free admission to a day of Championship or Sunday League cricket in 1995. I am sure that there have been examples of similar shambles on other sporting stages, but there can have been few on such an international scale. Some of the England players had travelled halfway across London; some of those from Australia, India, Pakistan, South Africa and the West Indies somewhere near halfway across the world. It could be some time before there is a further attempt to stage such an event in England.

Finally, a word about scoring with and for the Press. My only direct experience of 'for' rather than 'with' was on a rickety school examination desk in an even more rickety press box in St George's, Grenada, when England played their Easter fixture against the West Indies Board XI. Compared with the Trinidad Test which preceded it and the Barbados one which followed, it was a low key affair where England's heavy defeat, coming, as it did, immediately after their disastrous and spectacular 46 all out in the Port of Spain Test, represented the nadir of their fortunes on this trip. On this occasion, most of the press had emptied their invective on the England team, were happy to relax a little between more important fixtures and content with a minimum of statistics during and after play.

It is, however, an accepted part of the first-class cricket scene that scorers and Press work fairly closely together: at Lord's and the Foster's Oval, the Press usually have their own scorer, which reduces the number of enquiries to the official scorers, though they are usually asked to confirm details of hundreds, fifties, bowling figures, analysis of extras etc. At most grounds, however, the Press are more directly dependent on the official scorers and on some outgrounds, such as Guildford, the scorers share a tent with the Press. At Canterbury, the official scorers are situated at the front of the press box and on a number of grounds, fairly adjacent.

There are few problems about supplying statistics, but some scorers tend to get a little irritated when asked to do more than that and supply details of what happened in the first few overs before the journalists showed up or early in the afternoon session when they were still exploring the hospitality tents. There is some anecdotal evidence of minor contretemps between scorers and Press, when the former may see the latter as too demanding and the latter see the former as slow and unco-operative.

But, at the end of the day, scorers and Press need to work closely together and I have every admiration for those journalists who, having spent several hours drinking, eating and reminiscing about former matches, other matches taking place at the same time and every subject under the sun (or, indeed *The Sun*) manage, nevertheless, to dictate or Tandy a few hundred words at close of play to ensure the nation's breakfast tables have something on them which roughly approximates to what actually happened on the field of play.

Chapter Eight

The Scoreboard Story

In March 1993, I was part of the Leicestershire party which went to Jamaica for the dual purpose of pre-season training and playing a few pro–am matches. In one of these, I was fielding on the boundary against Trelawny on a country ground called Hampden. The morning shift at the adjacent sugar refinery finished at 2 p.m. and the afternoon 'gate' was well into four figures. The talk in the crowd was of the following day's general election. Nevertheless, although there was no scoreboard of any kind on the ground, the spectators behind me were aware of the score, the target and the overs remaining.

It was at one and the same time a reflection on the Jamaican idolisation of cricket and a throwback to what the situation must have been like in England before scoreboards became virtually universal. In the early days there was a quaint custom, whereby the scorers stood up when the scores were level – by which time presumably it was much too late for the fielding captain to change the tactics!

My first recollections of scoreboards (I was five at the time and the 1948 Australians were on tour in England) was at the Co-op Sports Ground in Barnsley, where my father used to play. The ground is situated just behind the better-known venue of Oakwell, home of Barnsley Football Club.

Technically, I suppose, it wasn't even a scoreboard: the practice was to hang tin plates – with the same digit on both sides – in the windows of what was the scorebox perched on top of the players' pavilion. In my days of developing numeracy, I became intrigued and perplexed that what read '52' from the inside read '25' from the outside; but experiments in my bedroom with number plates manufactured from corn-flake packets as I tried to follow Test match broadcasts on what was then the BBC Light Programme confirmed the consistency of the phenomenon.

My first scoreboard is no more. It has become a victim of progress, the space which it occupied being required for the expansion of the Barnsley Metrodome. Compared with many scoreboards on club and county grounds, the method was primitive, but it did at least have the advantage that what was showing on the outside could be ascertained from the inside – and there are many, many scoreboards, otherwise quite sophisticated, where that is not the case.

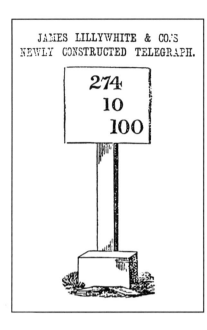

JAMES LILLYWHITE & CO.'S
NEWLY CONSTRUCTED TELEGRAPH.

274
10
100

James Lillywhite's
Telegraph, 1872 –
'manufactured with
all the latest
improvements. It
can easily be carried
about by the
Ground man, and is
so compact that the
whole of the figures
required for use can
be deposited in the
box at the bottom.'

The first 'telegraph' was introduced at Lord's in the year that scorecards were first sold there, namely 1846, and apparently the spectators were suitably impressed:

The scoring or telegraph board made its introduction at Lord's in 1846. It gave the total number of runs, the wickets down, and the score credited to the last man out. It was considered a great boon to those who frequented the ground, more so as the printing tent had not yet made its appearance. (1)

The Oval followed suit two years later and by 1872, James Lillywhite and Co.'s 'newly constructed telegraph' is being advertised in his eponymous *Cricketers' Annual*.

It is now 'manufactured with all the latest improvements. It can easily be carried about by the Ground man, and is so compact that the whole of the figures required for use can be deposited in the box at the bottom.'

There are advertisements in late nineteenth-century *Wisdens* for Cricket Telegraph Boards and Plates from Benetfink 'The Great City Cricket and Athletic Outfitter' and a firm by the name of Jeffries and Co. advertise a number of items of equipment including bats for the new game of lawn tennis in an advertisement which carries an illustration of a traditional scoreboard of the Total–Wickets–Last Player kind.

In 1876, the basic information of the 'telegraph' was supplemented in the

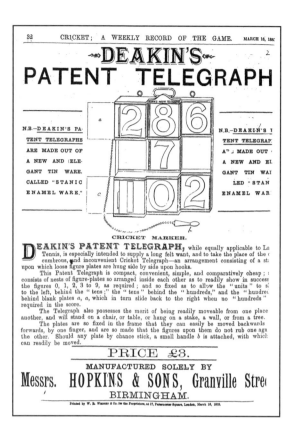

Deakin's Patent Telegraph, 1883 – '... will stand on a chair or table or hang from a tree'.

Kent v Gloucesterhire match at Canterbury in that the batsmen's names, arranged in the order of going in were placed on the telegraph board as they went in so that they could be seen from all parts of the ground. (2) Under 'Ironmonger for names of Players' the club accounts record a payment of £3. The practice has not survived.

The new technology of the 1880s saw a mini-revolution, when alongside advertisements for rollers, turnstiles and undervests, there appears in the year-old weekly *Cricket* on 16 March 1883 an advertisement proclaiming the advent and extolling the virtues of Deakin's Patent Telegraph. It was 'made out of a new and elegant tin ware called "stanic enamel ware"' and had an arrangement where the numbers did not hang on hooks, but compactly slid behind each other. The telegraph was movable and could be placed on a table, a chair or even hang on a tree. The plates could be moved backwards and forwards by one finger, but a small handle was provided in case they became stuck.

A year earlier, a new type of telegraph had accompanied the Australian touring party. First appearing at Oxford in their opening fixture on 15,16

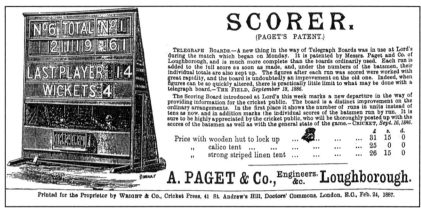

Paget's Patent Scorer, 1886 – 'A new way of providing information for the cricket public.'

and 17 May, it attracted the attention of the *Bell's Life* reporter:

> What appeared to be an excellent novelty was exhibited during the Oxford match, and that was a patent scoring board or cricket telegraph. The figures, which are very distinctly printed on canvas, work on rollers moved by small handles, in a similar way to that seen in office date-boxes. By this machine the tedious and slow process of hanging the loose iron plates is done away with, and there is a great saving of time and trouble. The new fashioned board which is the invention of Mr F. Dening of Chard, Somerset, was set up at Oxford beside the old machine, and before I knew anything about the idea, I noticed from the Pavilion how much more quickly and plainly the score was shown on one board than on the other. Everyone who saw it admitted the great improvement, and many wondered why no one had thought of the notion before. I have often been irritated by the delays in putting up the totals, and the new board can be worked instantaneously. (3)

That summer, Dening's invention was to impress the crowds at The Oval, Lord's, Cambridge and Taunton. It did not, however, display individual totals. That innovation had to wait until 1886 and the introduction of the Paget's Patent Scorer for the Testimonial Match for J.A. Murdoch, Assistant Secretary of MCC, when an England XI played the Australian touring team at Lord's on 13, 14 and 15 September. *Cricket*, in its 'Pavilion Gossip' column reports as follows:

> The scoring board introduced at Lord's this week in connection with Mr Murdoch's testimonial match, marks a new departure in the way of providing information to the cricket public, at least on English grounds. In Australia a *very*

elaborate system of scoring has been in vogue for some time and the game can be followed with the greatest ease by spectators. The invention of Messrs Page [sic] and Co., of Loughborough, follows something of the same lines, though as far as I am able to judge of the apparatus used in the Colonies, it does not go to anything like the same extent.

The board used this week, though, is a distinct improvement on the ordinary arrangements in England. In the first place it shows the number of runs in units instead of tens as now, and in addition notes the individual scores of the batsmen run by run. In some details it is sensible of improvement, but the general principle shows a great advance on anything seen in England as yet. When the idea is perfected, it is sure to be highly appreciated by the cricket public who will be thoroughly posted up with the scores of the batsmen as well as with the general state of the game. (4)

Suitably and subtly edited, these paragraphs formed the basis of advertisements for the new telegraph that appeared in *Cricket* the following February and in the 1887 edition of Lillywhite's *Cricketers' Annual*. The publicity includes quotations from *The Field* and *Scottish News* which points out that 'the figures are worked by cards and can be very rapidly altered' and adds as a PR touch that 'the new board would not interfere with the sale of cards (meaning scorecards in this case) as the spectator without a card would have no means of knowing the names of the batsmen.'

The latter may underestimate more than slightly the knowledge of the late Victorian cricket follower, as the accompanying drawing which almost certainly reflects the state of play at some stage, probably lunch time on the first day, shows England at 119 for 4 and no 1 at 61 not out. A glance at the details of the match in *Wisden* or *Scores and Biographies* indicates that no 1 was Mr W.G. Grace, who might just have been recognisable by the odd spectator!

In the small space that remains in the advertisement in Lillywhites there is publicity for the same company's 'Patent Garden Engine' which can be used when no water pressure is available for lawns, tennis and cricket grounds, conservatories etc., for carriage and horse washing and leaves both hands at liberty!

It was in 1902 that the first of the 'Deards' scoreboards advertisements appeared. The design was patented and the verbose style of turn-of-the-century publicity is again in evidence as the reader is informed of the advantages of Sam Deards' Patent Scoring Boards. The total is always above and stands out distinctly and there are nine sets of movable figures on rollers. It cannot get out of order or get stuck and a lad of 16 could easily work it. It is the cheapest and the figures stand out bold, being white on a dark blue ground. A number of county clubs endorse it.

There is an interesting footnote that 'In answer to many enquiries I wish to state that the Scoring Board lately erected at The Oval is not of my make'.

All counties will have their own scoreboard story: like the scorebook story, it would be tedious, time-consuming and doubtless go some way to proving the law of diminishing returns to research them all and, again, as in the case of scorebooks, the assumption may be made that two, in this case Surrey and Kent, are not atypical.

Surrey's board, to which the advertisement refers here, was in fact provided by Deards' contemporary competitor, Marshall Brothers of Nottingham, who appear to have cornered the market on the Test grounds with other boards at Headingley, Trent Bridge and Old Trafford. Its predecessor had stood on the gas-holder side of the ground since 1848 and by 1897 had been extended by the addition of batsmen's numbers and scores and bowlers' numbers as with Paget's Patent Scorer which had appeared at Lord's in 1886. Suggestions for additions to the board had been considered at the committee meeting of 21 July 1892 and were referred to the Ground Committee; suggestions for the admission of lady members considered at the same meeting were 'not entertained'. (5)

Photographic evidence suggests that a different board was in use in 1899 (6), but by 1900 the Ground Committee was seeking the opinions of other county secretaries on the scoreboards at their grounds and of the captain and scorer on various scoreboard designs, and a couple of weeks into the 1901 season the board which was to record the feats of Hayward, Hobbs, Sandham et al. was in place. (7) Four years later provision for the number of the catcher was made, but that apart, it stood virtually unchanged for half a century when it was replaced by the present board, the most efficient in the country according to the *Test Match Special* team and David Hopps who in the 1995 *Wisden* detects an element of romance in the solidity of this now obsolescent type of scoreboard:

> More than a decade has passed since computerised scoreboards began to change the face of English county grounds. For detailed information, the advantages of the best of them are undeniable, but if they remain for a century and more, they will never acquire the same solid and restful qualities of their manual predecessors. Wooden scoreboards, in all their alternative forms, help to form the character of the grounds they grace. (8)

On the other side of the ground there had been a small telegraph-type board adjacent to the old pavilion (9) and its successor (10) opened in 1898.

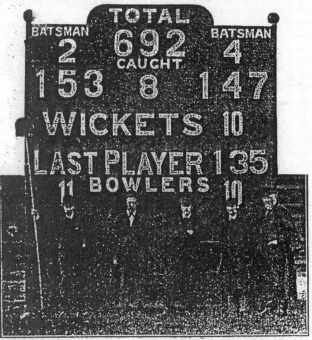

ADVANTAGES OF SAM DEARDS'
PATENT SCORING BOARDS.

The Total is always above, and stands out distinctly.
There are 9 Sets of movable figures on rollers.
It cannot get out of order, or get stuck.
A lad of 16 can easily work this board. It is the Cheapest.
The figures are on the surface of the board and stand out bold,
being white on a dark blue ground.

Already adopted and in use by the Essex, Worcester, Gloucester,
Leicester, and London County Clubs.

"It's a first-class board."—DR. W. G. GRACE.
"It's the best I've seen."—C. E. GREEN, ESQ.
"It's very good indeed, so simple."—LORD HAWKE.
"Your board has worked well, and given every satisfaction."—
F. C. TOONE, LEICESTER C.C.C.

N.B. In answer to many inquires I wish to state the Scoring Board lately erected
at the Oval is not of my make.

SAM DEARDS, Patentee, HARLOW.
LONDON OFFICE:—34, Old Broad Street, E.C.

Deards Scoreboard, 1902 – '... nine sets of movable figures on rollers'.

In 1920, this was superseded by the small additional board on the west side of the ground (this time it was one of Sam Deards' make) which survived until the 1980s when it was demolished to make way for the new Bedser stand.

While the technology for operating scoreboards has improved over the century, space-consuming wheels, drums and canvas belts yielding to more user-friendly electrically or mechanically operated flip-over numbers, the information displayed has changed astonishingly little and there has been often conscious and orchestrated opposition, perhaps fuelled by a desire to maximise revenue from scorecards, to the inclusion of any extra information.

In 1913, a suggestion had been put to the Surrey committee by a member that a board similar to that at Sydney – then and now light years ahead of anything in England – be installed. Again, along with various progressive suggestions through the years, it was 'not entertained'.(11) When in 1949, the design of a new scoreboard was considered, proposals to include the last innings score were rejected on the grounds that its inclusion might adversely affect the sale of scorecards. (12)

The requirements of players and umpires were clearly not factors to be taken into account. And in 1953, a *Times* leader, praising the virtues of anonymity, opposed the installation of fielders' indicator lights on the scoreboards at Lord's. (13) They had been in operation at The Oval for three years: ironically, except for international matches, they are not used today.

Back to Deards, however: by 1904, the disclaimer to The Oval board in his advertisements has gone and been replaced by 'This board is made in most convenient form for Export, and is in use in South Africa'.

Ten years later the form has changed somewhat. The publicity now begins: 'Do you want a good scoring board?' and Dr E.M. Grace joins his brother and Lord Hawke on a longer list of endorsers. The board is now in use at Canterbury, Maidstone, Hull and Liverpool and in 'the colonies'. London County, one of the earlier users, but by this time defunct, has surreptitiously been replaced by London County Council! We are now informed that 'The above can be recommended by Mr Sam Deards as a player and an *expert* of over 45 years on Cricket.'

Gerald Brodbribb has a page of photographs of historic scoreboards which includes Holmes and Sutcliffe at Leyton in 1932 in front of what is obviously a Deards board recording their celebrated 555 partnership. Other boards shown are a very similar one at Hove and 'black on white' ones at Trent Bridge and Northampton. I am not aware that any Deards scoreboards have survived, but I should be delighted to be proved wrong. The last 'black on white' one was at Canterbury, dating from 1928, now demolished and superseded by something electronic.

Sam Deards, however, is an interesting character in his own right. An

Deards scoreboard at Harlow Cricket Club – now derelict [Author's collection]

unpublished thesis (14) in the Harlow Public Library using Kelly's Directory as one of its major sources records that Samuel Deards was something of a local character and an energetic inventor of some note. In 1882 he was described as an 'Inventor and patenter of the centrifugal apparatus for greenhouses etc.' Four years later he had invented and patented the 'Victoria Dry Glazing', 50 tons or 60,000 feet of which was used at the Colonial and Indian Exhibition at South Kensington. He advertised this material as being 'well adapted for all railway, exhibition and conservatory roofs'. Also to his credit were patent coil boilers for churches, chapels, greenhouses, conservatories etc. Samuel Deards was still going strong in 1910 when he was making 'Smale's patent cement block-making machine'.

There is a photograph of Sam Deards's shop (15) the Bon Marché showing a wide range of goods and services advertised on the window and displayed on the pavement outside. Under the banner of Designers, Contractors, Gas Engineers, Machinists, Metal Workers and Ironmongers, Deards offers *inter alia* hot water, mechanics tools direct from Sheffield, baths, stoves and ranges.

As well as being captain of the local Fire Brigade, a post he held for 30 years, he was also Clerk to the Parish Council and an enumerator in the Population Censuses of 1881 and 1891. A 'Memory Corner' feature in the *Harlow Gazette and Citizen* in 1975 links the business with the glazing of the original Crystal Palace, but the dates do not tie in and material relating to its construction does not list him among the contractors.

Be that as it may, there is sufficient evidence about Deards's other activities to suggest that the manufacture of scoreboards was perhaps something of a sideline, a hobby converted into a job, but one pursued with the enthusiasm and professionalism associated with his other business and community activities.

The Deards family was involved with Harlow Cricket Club for several generations. Seagrave's thesis reports that cricket flourished in the district in the 1850s and 1860s and that Samuel Deards was Secretary of the club. As the Club Cricket Conference gives the date of establishment of the club as 1866, it is at least probable that he was one of the founder members.

Harlow were local league champions in 1899 and *The Book of Harlow* by local historian Ian Jones records that the club benefitted from Deards' invention of the familiar cricket scoreboard, the prototype of which was used at Marigolds Field. It is in fact still there or at least the shell of it is. It appears long abandoned and the old pavilion in which it is situated has been superseded by a modern structure and a modern scoreboard which ironically gives less information than its century-old predecessor which, despite its dereliction still clearly demonstrates the Deards-style layout of total above and batsmen's scores just below.

And from its humble beginnings at Marigolds Field, Harlow, the Deards scoreboard, as we have seen, became a fixture on county grounds at home and also in the 'colonies' and is featured in a number of photographs of scoreboards of significant cricketing occasions.

The minutes of the Managing Committee of the Kent County Cricket Club (16) in the early twentieth century record the installation of Deards scoreboards at Canterbury and later at Maidstone:

> With regard to the new scoring board Mr Deard [sic] had visited the Ground [Canterbury] and estimated that to fix one of his scoring-boards on the top of the members enclosure securely would cost £92 and he further recommended that in such an exposed position the back of it should be enclosed with woodwork instead of canvas and this would mean an additional expense of £10.

> In view of the increased cost it was decided to have a board at the Canterbury Ground only for this year at all events, and to submit plans for the erection of it to the Surveyor.

> The old board to be removed to the Tonbridge ground.

That was in February 1910; two years later a similar board was installed at Maidstone and by June it had been decided to have a door fitted at a cost of

Johnnie Walker scoreboard at Brighton, 1930 – Keeping holidaymakers informed [United Distillers Archive]

£2 5s 3d 'to keep boys and cattle from getting inside and interfering'.

The Deards board at Canterbury replaced one that had been in use for only three years. The minutes of 26 November 1906 record that:

> It was further decided that the new scoring board be fixed on the roof of the Members' Enclosure at the right hand corner, and that the figures be larger than those put up last year.

It was about the same time that the Report of the Young Players Committee for 1906 contained the following:

> The latest of them to join the Eleven, F. Woolley, is a young player of great promise, and the Committee are hopeful that he will be of great value to the County.

Not all boards were of the Deards style, however, and there was, of course a market for the simpler type 'telegraph' board for use in smaller clubs, schools etc., and an advertisement for a simpler board where the plates hang on and revolve around horizontal bars appears in one of the first editions of *The Cricketer* (4 June 1921). Called 'The "County" Scorer', patented and advertised alongside the 'Kachaball' Cricket Fielding Machine, its virtues are extolled in the following terms:

> The plates being fixed in position, cannot get lost. They cannot blow off in windy weather or get trodden on and made almost indecipherable through being constantly laid on the ground. Hanging as they do, the plates screen one another and consequently keep clean. Being always in position the board is ready at all times for immediate use without the necessity of collecting up and sorting out numbers as in the old system.

Most pre-war boards have now been replaced, though, even on the newer electronic boards, the information shown is considerably less than that shown before the war – before the Boer War in fact – on boards overseas, particularly Australia. The gradual disappearance of the Deards board from the county circuit has meant that while county clubs have tended to uniformity in the way of management structure, training methods, groundsmanship etc., they have become more diverse in the nature and layout of their scoreboards, which can cause some confusion for players, umpires, spectators and scorers if the section devoted to 'Overs' on one board is 'Batsman no 2' on another and 'Last Wicket Fell' on one is 'How Out' on another.

Essex get round this by having the same – literally the same – scoreboard on all home grounds but Chelmsford. It takes the form of a mobile scoreboard mounted on the side of a peripatetic pantechnicon van which has travelled the county's roads and graced its cricket grounds for well over 30 years and apart from a tendency to shed its numbers in high winds, this latter-day 'Deards on Wheels' is still going strong and has served its county and its members well.

SLR of Cossington, Leicestershire, the leading scoreboard design and manufacturing company has been instrumental in helping county and other clubs with updating their scoreboards, but has made no attempt to impose consistency. Different economies doubtless make such uniformity unachievable; perhaps too, the charm of variety makes it undesirable.

There is an interesting sideline in the history of scoreboards with the advent of the detailed Johnnie Walker ones in 1930. Not dissimilar in layout to the Australian boards mentioned earlier and discussed in more detail in the next chapter, these were different in that they were situated not at grounds but in seaside resorts and inland at Nottingham and Manchester, and although primarily a channel for the advertising of Johnnie Walker whisky, they provided a ball-by-ball service which was not to be available for many years from the BBC who had begun the live broadcasting of Test Matches only three years earlier. Perceived as a rival to the Press, they were constantly updated with information supplied by telephone from observers at the ground.

Their operation is described in the following contemporary record:

On the left of the Board are displayed the names of the batting side in black lettering. The two batsmen appear at the foot of the board and as they compile a score so their figures are shown against their name, a corresponding number being added to the side's total in the lower right-hand corner. In the event of a batsman being dismissed he re-appears on the batting list in red, whilst his score is placed against him on the left-hand side, the next batsman taking his place in the lower space.

The right hand side of the board is allotted to the fielding side. Here a notice 'fielded' is run up and down to indicate the player who has fielded each ball. An arrow with a red ball attached shows the bowler.

Undoubtedly the most interesting section of the board is the centre. Here is a metal plate painted green to represent the cricket ground on which are painted two wickets. A red and yellow disc represent the batsmen batting, these discs corresponding with similarly coloured discs, placed against the batsmens' [sic] names underneath.

Worcester

Taunton

Southampton (supplementary board)

Edgbaston

Stockton

Canterbury (now, alas, no more)

The Essex Mobile

Northampton

Cardiff (supplementary board)

Worcester (supplementary board)

Derby

Southport

Cardiff

Northampton (supplementary board)

Taunton

Guildford (supplementary board)

Harlow (minimalist compared with Deards)

Middlesbrough

Old Trafford

Adelaide Oval

Hove

Queens Park Oval, Trinidad

Chelmsford

Southampton

Guildford

Old Trafford

Chester-le-Street

Edgbaston

By an ingenious contrivance a white ball is suspended in front of the plate. The ball moves down the wicket to the batsman receiving the bowling, and then passes out to whatever part of the ground it has been hit to. The word 'fielded' moves up simultaneously against the name of the fielder and then the ball returns to the bowler... The fall of the wicket is indicated by a large notice 'OUT' falling across the batsman's total while the method of his despatch is displayed upon the right-hand side. This is a signal for tumultuous applause from the crowd should it be an Australian wicket and groans should an English wicket have fallen.

Huge crowds gathered in front of the scoreboards, on one occasion causing the trams to be stopped in Nottingham, and similar experiences elsewhere resulted in the notice 'Please keep back' being incorporated in the top right hand corner. (17)

The exercise was repeated for the 1934 tour and the cricket media were equally enthusiastic in their acclamation:

Until television really emerges from the laboratories, I do not think that there can possibly be invented a better method of watching 'distant' cricket than was provided during these Test matches by the special scoreboards erected at Great Yarmouth, Felixstowe, Southend, Margate, Ramsgate, Folkestone, Brighton, Hastings, Southsea and Weymouth. Many who read this article will undoubtedly have seen the boards at work themselves, but those who may not be interested in this short description of the manner in which it is controlled, and many of those who have stood for hours in front of it – getting the authentic Test Match thrill – may learn that it is neither wireless, nor 'electricity' that works the board ...

... Practically every move in the game as it occurs on the ground is faithfully reproduced by an ingenious mechanism, and it requires five operators who have to be fully trained in their work and must be able dramatically to interpret cricket. The difference between fast and slow and even googly bowling can be indicated by the manner in which the ball is manipulated. It is easy to see when batsmen attempt a run and then scurry back to their creases. Even such finer points as starting to run and then the ball crossing the boundary, making it unnecessary for the batsmen to cross over at all, and quick and accurate throwing in by the fielders – all these points are brought out. In fact, many of the thousands who watch these boards lose after a time any feeling that they are watching a mechanical representation of the game. Cheers and claps greet Don Bradman's dismissal; Hendren's half-century brings up cries of 'Good old Patsy'! (18)

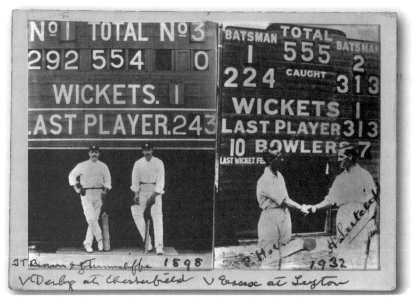

The Deards board at Leyton in 1932 records Holmes and Sutcliffe's breaking Brown and Tunnicliffe's 1898 record [Yorkshire County Cricket Club]

It is axiomatic that a good scoreboard should provide the public with relevant and useful information about the match in progress at the time, but one of the paradoxes of the electronic boards at both Lord's and The Oval is that they are capable of storing all kinds of information, but less capable of displaying it. If a detail of last year's Test Match is required, then the primary source is the scoresheet for the match and there is a variety of secondary sources such as newspapers, magazines and *Wisden*. The computerised memory of the scoreboard is not the obvious place most researchers would start looking.

The capacity to print out bowling figures, batsmen's times and bowler's economy rates is a sophisticated, but superfluous feature of the new board at Lord's and the downside is that it seems incapable of conveying basic information such as the score and overs remaining. In its brief life, it has had more glitches than the Mir spacestation. In the 1997 Varsity match, it was abandoned and the old manual board wheeled on from the Nursery Ground; in the Benson and Hedges Cup Final, as Surrey strolled to an easy victory, the capacity crowd found more entertainment in the eccentricities of the scoreboard, which struggled to get individual scores right, than in the progress of the match; and in the Middlesex–Surrey Championship fixture, it seemed totally incapable of changing the overs remaining from 36 to 35 without being virtually reprogrammed. Finally, at least for the time being, having correctly recorded one run for a wide in the National Club and Village Finals, it then found difficulty in counting the same infringement as two in the subsequent Championship match. In olden times, the 'Ground man' would simply have changed a 'tin' on his telegraph or Sam Deards would have moved his roller on by the appropriate number.

Even the most up-to-date scoreboards in England tend to be silent on the falls of previous wickets and current bowling figures, which are a standard feature on the boards of the Test grounds – and many others – overseas.

The only comparable board in England used to be at Trent Bridge, though that has now given way to a board that is less informative, but still has more on it than virtually anywhere else in the land. It operated from 1951 to 1973 when economics caused it to be abandoned. It is absolutely understandable that installation and renovation of scoreboards and expanding the information contained on them should be low on the shopping list of county clubs and come way behind expenditure on the team, the playing area and spectator facilities. On the other hand, the monster Melbourne scoreboards were financed by gate receipts and required only four operators and their electronic successors funded entirely from sponsorship.

In the age of the information explosion when satellite television provides instant statistical information on everything from darts to baseball and updates batting and bowling averages instantaneously, is it not a false economy to minimise the information provided? The situation is different in Australia, South Africa and elsewhere and it is to a somewhat different and more advanced scoreboard history that we now turn.

Chapter Nine

The Scoreboard Story – Australian Style

I do, however, counsel very urgently the need for up-to-date scoring boards of the Australian type on your principal grounds. I have just been reading an article in a leading English cricket publication by a very well-known writer. He was describing the happenings in an important match at Lord's. After telling of a glorious innings by a young player he wrote: 'I had no idea of his identity – there were no score-cards around at the time.' Subsequently, he told how he discovered the player's name.

Such a state of affairs to an Australian enthusiast is hard to comprehend. I am well aware of the forceful arguments regarding the revenue produced from selling score-cards, but I submit that 10,000 spectators who do not need score-cards to tell them what is happening are going to be a happier and more virile advertisement for the game than 8,000 who do. Cricket needs to retain its present followers and to gain new ones. Modern scoring-boards would be a big help, and any temporary loss would be recouped eventually through the turnstiles.

Modern? It could be, but for those attendance figures which rather give the game away. It was in fact Don Bradman in an article entitled 'Cricket at the Cross Roads' in the 1939 edition of *Wisden*. It is accompanied by contrasting photographs of the Sydney board in 1929–30 showing New South Wales 7 for 752 with Bradman 447 not out on his way to 452 and The Oval board of Hutton's record 364.

Since Bradman's time of course, we have seen the advent of the electronic scoreboard with detailed statistics on run rates required and similar indigestible information changing every ball.

The history of scoreboards in Australia is parallel chronologically to that in England, but technologically and in the way of information displayed, starts at a point further ahead in the late nineteenth century than that which most English boards have reached at the end of the twentieth. As mentioned in the previous chapter, boards in 'the colonies' have always been some way in advance. Photographic evidence suggests that there was a scoreboard at Melbourne in 1875, that it had possibly been repositioned by 1878 and been subject to some modernisation in time for the first 'Ashes' tour of 1882–83. The captain, the Hon. Ivo Bligh, was clearly impressed:

> The new scoring board, by which the whole score as taken down in the book, with the exception of the analysis of the bowling, is presented to the spectators was made use of in this match. (1)

Perhaps, as suggested in earlier chapters, the display of batting information before bowling information reflects the predominance given to batting over bowling and the class distinctions of an English society of which that in the Antipodes was a pale reflection. Bowling figures were soon to catch up, however.

Maurice Golesworthy (2) erroneously dates the installation of this board as 1884 – and is also two years adrift in his mention of the installation of the Paget Board at Lord's dating its introduction as 1884 rather than 1886 – but the evidence of the Bligh quotation and of the Melbourne Cricket Club archivist dates it as January 1883. Certainly the photographic evidence is that two new wings have been added by 1895 and the whole structure placed on top of a shelter.

Notwithstanding the slight uncertainties over precise dates, it is abundantly clear that, although approximately contemporary with the installation of the Paget board at Lord's, the Melbourne board was then, as now, light years ahead in terms of the information contained on it. From this point, the scoreboard story in Australia is one aspect of the battle for supremacy between Melbourne and Sydney.

Across the state boundary, Sydney was catching up:

> The SCG Trust chairman Phillip Sheridan, eager to expand membership, instructed Ned Gregory three weeks before the New South Wales-Victoria match in 1896 to build a scoreboard to replace the mounted board that showed only the individual scores of the batting side, name of the bowler and the sides' totals. Gregory had been pestering the Trust for years to improve the board and had his own design ready. In three weeks he had erected a board 20 metres wide and three metres high which sat on top of a 28-metre refreshment room. Numbers and letters each half a metre high were printed on calico and moved into position on brass rollers. It became one of the wonders of cricket. (3)

Ned Gregory was Curator at the SCG and it was not only for its size and mechanics that his invention was striking. The Sydney board was the first full detailed scoreboard in the tripartite spreadsheet layout (forgive the anachronism) of match details and scores of batsmen at the wicket, flanked by the batting scorecard and bowling figures which became, albeit with a number of variations, the prototype on most Test grounds outside the UK:

> Due to its orderly columns of words and numbers, it called to mind a densely-inscribed ledger of indisputable accuracy. Horizontally-hinged hopper doors or 'shutters' were available to retain every number for which a roller was not more suitable. The pointing hand which could be winched up and down the list of bowlers, similarly advanced the technology of scoring on a grand scale. (4)

The argument as to whether Melbourne or Sydney should be the capital of the new Commonwealth of Australia, established in 1901, was settled by the creation of Canberra; but the battle of the scoreboards continued, Melbourne taking a step ahead in the same year by opening a second board. The new one was the brainchild of Messrs H. Spowers and E. Symonds, opened at the beginning of the 1901–2 season at a cost of £907 14s 9d, an outlay recovered from the gate receipts generated by the England tour that summer. Having seen nothing more advanced than the 'Paget' (even the functional and later almost ubiquitous 'Deards', which sold at about a tenth the price, had not yet hit the market), the tourists were suitably impressed.

P.F. Warner on the following 1903–4 tour wrote:

> The Melbourne Cricket Ground with its huge scoring-board, or rather building, for it is of stone and red brick, on which every run with the bowler's analysis, and the manner of the batsman's dismissal is shown, is far superior to anything we have at home. (5)

More than 90 years later, it still is.

The information displayed on the Spowers board was not dissimilar from that on its counterpart at Sydney, though it was differently arranged, the batting statistics being displayed on the left and the bowling on the right. It is perhaps significant, however, that unlike boards in England, batting and bowling figures are from this point given equal prominence. In addition, the Sydney colour scheme was reversed, the Melbourne colours being white on a black background, but the same ledger-like layout is evident and there were the additional innovations of spring-tensioned rollers and a 'how out' column in which were entered 'C 1', 'B 2' etc.

Sydney's rejoinder in 1904 was to dismantle and re-erect the Gregory board higher up the Hill, to transfer the fall of wickets column from the left to the right of the board and use the resulting space for racing results. The

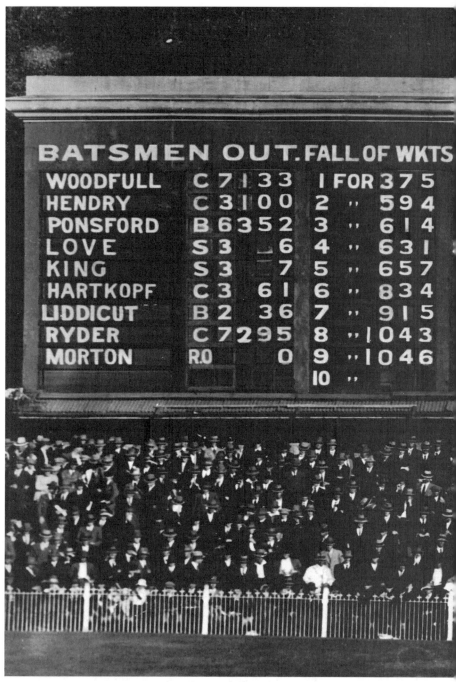

The monster Melbourne board shows Victoria's record 1,107 against New South Wales in 1926

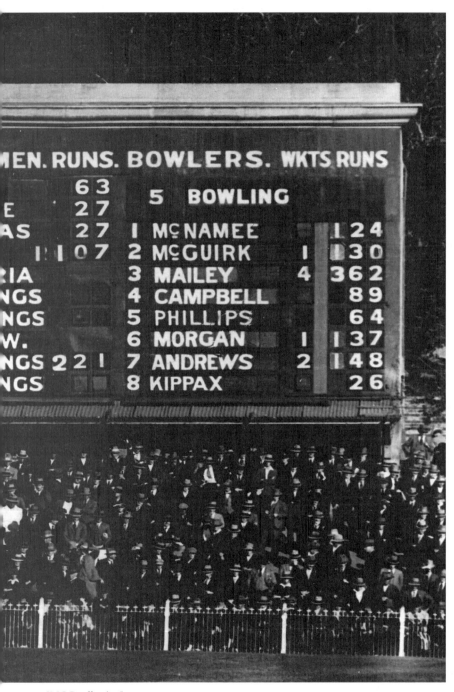

MEN.	RUNS.	BOWLERS.	WKTS	RUNS
	63	5 BOWLING		
E	27			
AS	27	1 McNAMEE		124
	107	2 McGUIRK	1	130
RIA		3 MAILEY	4	362
NGS		4 CAMPBELL		89
NGS		5 PHILLIPS		64
W.		6 MORGAN	1	137
NGS	221	7 ANDREWS	2	148
NGS		8 KIPPAX		26

[MCG collection]

numbers were changed to white on black backgrounds, the names remaining in their original format.

Unable to improve the quality and quantity of information on the Sydney board, Melbourne responded in 1907 by opening a second board on the other side of the ground. The archivist reports two boards in 1901, but the likelihood is that these were the new one installed that year and the earlier one, on the front of the old Stable and Cart House, the latter being superseded by the no 2 board.

The two Melbourne boards operated in tandem until 1925 when the no 1 board was demolished. The no 2 board was dismantled and resited in 1936 adjacent to the new Southern Stand. After a further move in 1955 it was eventually dismantled in 1981, yielding to the march of time and technology and being replaced by a state-of-the-art electronic board. The faithful old servant was not consigned to the knacker's yard, however. It was transported to Canberra where it became the Fingleton Scoreboard and began a new lease of life at the Manuka Oval in January 1983.

Perhaps the best known photograph of the no 2 scoreboard at Melbourne is that showing Victoria's 1,107 in 1926–27, with the falls of the eighth and ninth wickets at 1,043 and 1,046 respectively, as well as Mailey's 4 for 362. It is surely a matter of congratulation for the scorers and scoreboard operators that both batting and bowling figures do seem to add up to 1,107.

Meanwhile, back in Sydney, Ned Gregory's board was considered obsolete within 30 years.

The new scoreboard at the back of the SCG hill where it did not obscure the view of many spectators as the old board had, proved one of the successes of the 1924–25 season. (6) Soon afterwards the board was fitted with electric lights, so that the bowler, the batsman on strike and fielder could be identified. That too, has now been superseded by an all-singing, all-dancing electronic monster and stands redundant, forgotten and obscured by the Doug Walters stand at the back of what has now been renamed Yabba's Hill.

Adelaide opened its board in the 1911–2 season, following a report from the Chairman of the South Australian Cricket Association's Building Committee in October 1909:

> Subject to a favourable agreement being entered into with the SA Football League, this Committee is of an opinion that the time is opportune for the erection of a Members' Pavilion and Scoring Board, and further suggests that the cost of same be raised by the issue of debentures.

It replaced earlier versions somewhat more primitive than its contemporaries in New South Wales and Victoria:

Although periodic overhauls had improved the black-on-white apparatus as it stood in December 1893 – when attendants with paste brushes posted the players' names like bills on a hoarding – in fact it had become no more than an enlargement in a reversed colour scheme of the same eyesore. For example, on an occasion exactly seven years later in 1900 when Clem Hill compiled his record-breaking innings of 365, one can see that ill-spelled, hand-painted names on canvas-covered planks had replaced the job-lot jumble of giant woodblock labels. And closer scrutiny reveals that, together with the bank of 'rollers' giving the running totals, the equally fatigued panel listing the strikers of the batting side had been meanly recycled. (7)

The layout and technical features of the icon that replaced these primitive structures were derived from those of the no 2 board at Melbourne, with the principal exception that the totals and scores of the batsmen at the wicket were, at Adelaide, on the left, not the centre, panel of the three. There have been minor modifications of layout, such as the introduction of a bowling indicator, numbering of the fielding side to enable catchers to be included in the dismissal details and provision for the number of overs bowled and remaining; but these relatively minor modifications and the superimposition of advertising material apart, the information displayed has survived virtually intact until the present day.

The installation did not meet with universal acclaim. After the South Australia–MCC match of 1911–2, Pelham Warner was far less complimentary than he had been about its Melbourne role model eight seasons earlier and critical of the SACA's priorities:

> The outfield is not in keeping with the pitch. Possibly not enough money is spent on the ground itself, and to an outsider £1500 seems a large amount to spend on a colossal scoring board, with a bar beneath, which shuts out a view of the cathedral, when a quarter of that sum could well be applied to making the outfield smoother. (8)

The bar is still there and the cathedral is still quite visible from most vantage points.

The Adelaide board was replicated at the WACA, Perth, but the format amended in 1990 to place the key details on the central panel.

The Mitsubishi Diamond Vision Mk I Screen was installed at the MCG in 1982 to be replaced a decade later at a cost of $A7.3m, funded entirely by sponsorship arrangements, by the larger Mk III version, claimed by the manufacturers to be the most up-to-date outdoor display video screen available. At the time it was the fourth of its kind in the world, the other three

Adelaide scoreboard, 1893 – South Australia v New South Wales [MCG collection]

The current Adelaide board – erected 1911 and still going strong, showing Hookes–Phillips record partnership of 462 (unbroken) for South Australia v Tasmania 1987 [Adelaide Oval Museum]

being at the Tokyo Dome, Tokyo Racecourse and the Dodgers Stadium, Los Angeles. With a screen size of 17.28 m x 6.4 m it is 40 per cent larger than the screen it replaced and some 100 times the size of the Lillywhite Telegraph, though interestingly about the same size as Ned Gregory's monster board at the SCG almost a century earlier and somewhat smaller than the one at the Adelaide Oval. There is no way this one can be easily carried about by the 'Ground man' – or indeed either of them, for in 1994, the history of 1907 was repeated and a second screen installed on the opposite side of the ground.

The triple purpose of supplying detailed statistical information, instant action replays and advertisements is certainly an excellent service for spectators and sponsors, though perhaps less so for players and umpires; but there are occasions when there is a clash of interests, especially perhaps at the end of an over when players, spectators, umpires, official scorers even, may need to check the score only to find the state-of-the-art screen advertising the local beer, Chinese restaurant or furniture warehouse down the road.

Mike Ringham, scorer on three Australian tours of England, while impressed by electronic boards, considers it unfortunate that the operators tend to regard the match as subordinate to their statistics and is strongly of the opinion that the same screen should not be used for scores, replays and advertisements. Ian Wooldridge was certainly not impressed by the apparatus installed at Lancaster Park, Christchurch to supplement the razzmatazz surrounding Limited Overs International cricket in New Zealand:

> The electronic scoreboard, presumably installed to apprise patrons of such fundamental information as the current total appeared to have some anarchic mind of its own.

> Every time you looked at it, it flashed jerky pictographs of a thick-thighed high-kicking lady dancer or conundrum messages reading 'crop a cop'... Then, as you expected it to declare the required run-rate, it announced: 'Happy birthday, Norm Withers'... (9)

Certainly, there is a danger, as with computerisation generally, to slip into the trap of information overload and to display information simply because it is readily available and one is driven to reflect on shifting balances between cricket *per se* and its peripheral commercialisation when one learns, for example that the computerised scoreboard installed by the Transvaal Cricket Association at the Wanderers Stadium in Johannesburg has one PC to score the match and two to capture information not generated by the match, such as career statistics, advertisements, messages and animations for fours, sixes, wickets, dropped catches etc. (10)

Technologically, however, the boards – if one can still call them boards rather than mega-pixel hypermonitors – at Sydney, Melbourne and Brisbane and on most of the South African grounds are outstanding and one can only commend the initiative of the authorities at McLean Park, Napier, New Zealand of acquiring second-hand and adapting the electronic scoreboard that had been used at the 1994 Winter Olympic Games in Lillehammer. There is an interesting and unusual variation at Green Park, Kanpur, where a large 'M' with six lights incorporated shows the number of balls bowled so far in an over, then the whole of the 'M' lights up at the end of the over if it happens to be a maiden.

All ICC members but England have in general followed the detailed information pattern and tripartite spreadsheet layout of Australian boards rather than the English minimalist approach. Many – especially in the West Indies and the sub continent – are little more than wooden frames on to which the details are slid into grooves or hung on nails. The twentieth century is now too far advanced for England to have the time to bring its scoreboards into it, but the approaching millennium does at least provide an opportunity for a shortcut from the nineteenth century to the twenty-first.

Chapter Ten

Scorecards

The revenue generated by the sale of these cards of varying format, size and thickness has been advanced in the last two chapters as one of the reasons for the slow progress of information contained on English scoreboards. The link may be somewhat tenuous, but it remains the case that buying a scorecard, filling it in and retaining it as a permanent souvenir of a day at the cricket is a well-established custom – albeit perhaps a dying one that is peculiar to a decreasing proportion of a decreasing total of English followers.

The *Wisden Book of Cricket Memorabilia* implies that there is a parallel between scorecards as cricketing ephemera and love letters as social ephemera, evoking as they do memories of a bygone age and reducing in number and popularity alongside other, more sophisticated forms of communication. Certainly the practice prevalent in the late nineteenth and earlier twentieth centuries of printing complete match cards on silk and nostalgically cherishing them does nothing to detract from the analogy.

We have seen in Chapter One that the earliest surviving scorecard can be traced to 1773 and continues the bifurcation between scoring a match and maintaining a permanent record begun in 1744 with the Kent v All England match. The 1773 card, the first traceable one of T. Pratt, the Sevenoaks Vine scorer and printer was of a 'Grand Match on Sevenoaks Vine ... Hambledon Club with Yalden against England.' The latter with 177, against totals of 77 and 49, won by an innings and 51 runs. It was long before the days of bowling analyses, indeed long before the days when bowlers received credit for taking wickets by any method other than bowled; but there are indications from other sources (1) that later cards were updated at lunchtime and indeed at the fall of each wicket. A century or so later, in 1886 MCC resolved that a card be posted on the notice boards at the Pavilion at the fall of every wicket. (2) Such services are no longer provided, having now been overtaken by Ceefax, Teletext and other forms of immediate communication.

The woodcut surmounting Pratt's card shows an underarm bowler, wickets with two stumps, an umpire at each end and what appears to be an astonishingly orthodox five-four field. The notchers are situated discreetly in the extra cover area.

Interestingly, all the Hambledon Club are given initials (albeit a single one, one forename being the norm in the eighteenth century). Of the England team, six players are given initials, in four cases to distinguish them from another of the same surname, and five are designated by their surname only. Is it that the compiler of the scorecard did not know their initials or do we have an early rudimentary example of professionals being distinguished from amateurs in a way that was to persist for almost two centuries?

Maurice Golesworthy (3) and H.S. Altham (4) place Pratt's first card at 1776, a date also used by Robert Brooke (5) who suggests the first printed cards were for Hampshire v Kent at Broadhalfpenny Down on 3-5 July of that year.

The Sevenoaks card, however, is clearly dated 1773 and the programme for the Bicentenary Week of Sevenoaks Vine Cricket Club, celebrated in 1934, notes that the block from which the card was produced was used for many years after 1773 and may well have been used for many years before, although no earlier cards are known and the block itself is now lost.

Pre-1773 cards may have existed, but there is no firm evidence and Brooke suggests that 'although reproduced as genuine in some books they are in fact modern fakes based on a collection of old scores published in 1862'.

The *Wisden Book of Cricket Memorabilia*, however, records sightings of scorecards in 1772 and reports that:

> ... scorecards carried asterisks and other printer's rules to indicate the method of dismissal: out of their ground, run out, catched out [sic] and bowled out. The next year scorecards specified who were the bowlers, the wicketkeeper and that most indispensable of fielders, long stop as well as the earliest use of the word 'byes', instead of the older 'bye-runs' or 'bye-balls'.

If that is so, it was a further 150 years before the wicket-keeper was regularly designated again. Towards the end of the nineteenth century, there is often an indication as to the identity of the captain, but it is not until the 1920s that the familiar dagger begins to appear against the wicket-keeper and the asterisk against the captain – except at Lord's where there was and remains the reverse tradition of a dagger for the captain and asterisk for the wicket-keeper.

Golesworthy suggests that the Pratt card was an isolated example, there being no more until Frederick Lillywhite introduced his portable printing press to the game in 1846. There is evidence, however, that Pratt printed the scores of the Hambledon Club's matches between 1777 and 1788, albeit on flimsy pieces of paper rather than cards, although these were *ex post facto* records rather than the nineteenth-century type which enabled spectators to keep their own records of the principal details of the score. (6)

There is also a card of a match between Hampshire with Ring and Aylward

GRAND MATCH on SEVENOAKS VINE. 1773.

HAMBLEDON CLUB with YALDEN against ENGLAND.

HAMBLEDON CLUB	First	Second		ENGLAND	First
T. Brett ....B by Lum	26	C by Mins 1		J. Miller...........C by Barb	73
G. Leer ....run out	14	not out 15		Simmons ....B—Brett	20
T. Sueter ....B—Lum	11	C—Lum 9		T. May ....B—Barb	16
P. Stewart ....run out	5	B—Wood 0		Minshull...........hit wicket	15
W. Yalden ....B—Wood	5	B—Lum 0		J. Wood .. ..B—Hogs	14
J. Aylward ....C—Mins	4	B—Lum 13		T. Wood ....B—Hogs	12
W. Hogsflesh........C—Sim	4	C—Wood 0		R. May...............not out	10
J. Small sen........C—Lum	3	run out 4		T. White...........B—Nyren	7
R. Nyren..........C—White	2	C—Mins 5		Pattenden...........C—Hogs	1
E. Aburrow ....not out	2	B—Lum 2		Lumpy ....B—Brett	6
W. Barber ......B—R. May	1	B—Wood 0		Child...............B—Hogs	1
Bye Runs..	0	Bye Runs 0		Bye Runs..	2
Total....	77	49		Total....177	

The oldest known surviving scorecard – Hambledon v England at Sevenoaks Vine 1773
[Sevenoaks Vine Cricket Club]

against England played on Windmill Downs in 1791 for a purse of a thousand guineas. Most of the players are designated by surname only, though four have initials, three are 'John' and there is one 'Sen', one 'Esq' and one Colonel. It is printed by T. Cane of Earls Court, Leicester Fields. (7)

The *Wisden Book of Cricket Memorabilia* also mentions scorecards of 1803, 1817, 1824, 1840 and 1843 and refers to Ashley-Cooper's view that scorecards were issued at Brighton in 1823 (Altham agrees with Brighton, specifying the Gentlemen v Players match, but gives the date as 1838), to Rockley Wilson, a scorecard collector who records a card printed by T. Orton of Sheffield in 1827 and to cards advertised for sale, dated 1837, 1838 and 1839. There are also records of cards for Kent v England in 1839 and 1841 and Sussex v England in 1847. (8)

So it appears that there was a spasmodic and chequered history of scorecards before they appeared at Lord's in 1846 (9) shortly after the 'telegraph' was installed. Until that time, their nearest equivalents were the match bills advertising forthcoming matches and the anticipated teams in a similar way to theatre bills. It is from 1846, however, with the introduction of Frederick Lillywhite's press and printing tent that the scorecard story really takes off and becomes a commercial venture as Lillywhite's peripatetic equipment moved from ground to ground and even went on the tour of the USA and Canada in 1859.

By 1854, the cards are advertising that:

LILLYWHITE's Printing Tent is under the distinguished patronage of the Marylebone Club, at whose matches it is in attendance as well as others of notoriety. Cards are Printed and issued on the ground, where a statement of the game &c. can always be obtained. Each day's play of the grand matches forwarded by post to 'season Subscribers' of which Officials of Clubs will derive the advantage of [sic] by purchasing at a small amount at Lillywhite Bros Manufactory, 10, Princes Terrace, Caledonian Road, Islington, London, where an extensive stock of Cricket-ng [sic] Articles may always be inspected. Send for List of Prices, – Clubs or Trade; Scores sent by post. (10)

By 1865, the 'distinguished patronage' has been extended to include Sussex County Cricket Club and other counties, and the advertising includes not only Lillywhite's own products (*Scores and Biographies, Guide to Cricketers*) and cricket clothing, but also G.F. Salter and Co., Dyers, Cleaners, Bleachers of 67, Western Road, Hove.

From this point, advertising begins to creep in and to form an integral part of scorecards and of county clubs' income from them, although the cards themselves vary considerably in size, format and the amount of information carried. Brodribb mentions that those sold at Leyton included the number of boundaries and also the scores in other matches (as did those at Lord's and some other grounds) and has an example of a card issued at Brabourne Stadium, Bombay for an India XI v Commonwealth XI match which indicates which batsman was out at the fall of each wicket and also the time in and time out of each. (11) In 1930, so swift were the printers at updating scorecards that Strudwick was able to write:

> "... as each batsman is dismissed, you must mark his score and the method of his dismissal down on your own card. If you do not like the trouble of doing that, you have usually only to wait a few minutes and the enterprising printer will have brought out the latest score-card with full details up to date. (12)

The advent and increased use of public address systems to provide both match and advertising information has seen a decline in the importance of scorecards in the same way, I suppose, as the telephone has reduced the incidence of those love letters.

At The Oval, and doubtless elsewhere, the practice in the nineteenth century was for a printer to purchase the right to print and sell cards on the ground, though the club exercised control over what was printed on them. In 1872, the offer of Messrs Merser and Gardner, who also printed the Club's scorebooks, was accepted, subject to details of approaching matches being included on the front of the card; in 1873 improvements were suggested, but Mr Gardner did not feel disposed to increase the expense of producing cards by the inclusion of telegraphic news and in 1874, the printers signified their intention to discontinue, leaving the way open for the Secretary to open negotiations with other printers. He was instructed by the Committee carrying the resolution unanimously to secure the 'best possible terms, no less sum than £40 to be accepted.' (13)

The card for the 1880 Test match is printed by Merser and Sons, but by the turn of the century, Merritt and Hatcher have a firm hold on the contract for printing scorecards, the cost having risen to £105 by 1898, (14) though there was in 1895 a resolution, subsequently rescinded and in 1897 a suggestion, not acted upon, that the club should print its own and in 1899 the offer of a printing press. The arrangement, though subject to annual renewal, continued up to and after the First World War when in 1919, the minutes record that:

> It was decided to grant the exclusive right of printing and selling score cards at the Oval in 1919 to Merritt and Hatcher Ltd, the rent to be paid to be based on the average profits for the years 1911, 1912 and 1913 when the Club received £175 annually.

> It was agreed (a) that the Club should provide 6 Ground Boys on County Match days to sell score cards and that no cards should be printed on days other than

County Match days, except at the express wish of the Committee (b) that the charge for scorecards in 1919 should be twopence each. (15)

From 1921, cards were printed on all match days and in 1927 the split of profits from cards was changed to 50:50 from 57.2 per cent to the printers and 42.8 per cent to the Club. One can only speculate as to what kind of discussion must have gone on in committee before those percentages were arrived at! In 1932, Wightman & Co. took over from Merritt and Hatcher (16) and for the first time, advertising was included on the backs of the cards.

It was suggested in the first chapter that social history was reflected in cricket history which in turn is reflected in scoring. Perhaps nowhere is this more clearly crystallised than in the way in which names are presented on scorecards. We have seen that on Pratt's Hambledon v England scorecard, the Hambledon players had initials and most of the England players did not. Lillywhite's practice was to give all players initials and to follow the names of the amateurs with 'Esq' or precede them with 'Hon', 'Rev' or whatever. Umpires have surnames only; scorers are not mentioned.

By the time MCC are printing their own cards, the differences are more pronounced and epitomised in the Gentlemen v Players matches. The Gentlemen have full initials and 'Esq', although when in 1874, 12 of MCC played 18 of America at Lord's, the MCC were Esquires but the Americans weren't. The Players had surnames only, this distinction continuing the practice of the former match bills and becoming the standard procedure on most scorecards up to the time of the Second World War. Nottinghamshire cards featured 'Wild' and 'Daft'. Some would say things have not changed a great deal.

Julius Caesar of Surrey is given his full name, but this practice is not entirely consistent. For instance, amid the Esquires in the Surrey team which played Notts at The Oval in 1878, we find:

Lane
H Jupp
Richard Humphrey
Barratt

Where professionals shared a surname, it was the practice to give the initials in brackets after the name; thus the Nottinghamshire line-up against Sussex in 1925 – and doubtless many other fixtures – was:

1. Gunn (G)
2. Whysall

3. Gunn (J)

4. A W Carr (Capt)

The system certainly reflects a class-consciousness which has now disappeared from first-class cricket, but still exists to an extent in society and lower down the cricketing scale in fancy hat' and similar sides. In presenting the ten-year statistics which are discussed in Chapter Eleven, the Editor of *Cricket* feels constrained to write:

> It may be worth while to mention that the sole reason why I have given the amateurs' names thus: F S Jackson and the professionals' thus: Sugg (F H) is that it may be possible to distinguish at a glance to which section any particular cricketer belongs, and not at all because I believe in any necessary inevitable and natural inferiority of the professional cricketer, a class worthy of the respect of all men. (17)

The lady doth protest too much? Even in the denial of the assumed superiority of the amateur is a strong recognition of the divisiveness that was to characterise first-class cricket until well into the twentieth century.

After the Second World War, on scorecards at Lord's and The Oval the practice was modified and professionals' initials were included *after* the surname. So, for instance, in the 1961 Test Match at Lord's, the England line up begins:

1. Pullar G

2. R Subba Row

3. E R Dexter

4. P B H May

5. M C Cowdrey

6. Barrington K F

The distinction between amateur and professional dressing rooms was abolished at Lord's after the First World War, but not the social niceties. As Geoffrey Moorhouse recalls:

> It is well remembered that just before a Middlesex match began ... a loudspeaker announcement advising team changes made one other correction to the printed scorecard. 'For F.J. Titmus, read Titmus, F.J.' it said. On such minutiae did a whole segment of English social history depend. (18)

The Australian side – all notionally amateurs – had their initials before.

INTERNATIONAL
CRICKET TOURNAMENT.

AT THE

GERMANTOWN CRICKET GROUNDS, PHILADELPHIA.

Official Score Card.

2.30 P.M. Third Day—September 15th, 1875. 5 Cts.

FIRST MATCH—CANADA VS. PHILADELPHIA.

PHILADELPHIA.

FIRST INNINGS.		SECOND INNINGS.	
Geo. M. Newhall, run out	4	c. Kearney, b. Eberts	30
F. E. Brewster, c. Spragge, b. Eberts	8	c. Powell, b. M'Lean	8
John Hargreaves, c. Powell, b. Kearney	13	b. Eberts	0
R. S. Newhall, hit wicket b. Kearney	5	c. Spragge, b. Whelan	24
John Large, run out	18	b. Greenfield	30
D. S. Newhall, c Spragge, b. Whelan	1	st. Armstrong, b. Greenfield	5
Thos. Hargreaves, c. Spragge, b. Eberts	32	c. Armstrong, b. Whelan	0
R. N. Caldwell, b. Eberts	10	c. Kearney, b. Eberts	0
R. L. Baird, b M'Lean	11	b. Eberts	5
Chas A. Newhall, leg bef. wicket b. Eberts	0	b. Eberts	5
Robt. Pease, not out	2	c. Brodie, b. M'Lean	1
Spencer Meade, b. M'Lean	4	not out	0
Byes 4, Leg byes 3, Wides 2	9	Byes 2, Leg byes 2, Wides 2	6
Total	117	Total	114

CANADA.

FIRST INNINGS.		SECOND INNINGS.	
F. W. Armstrong, b. C. A. Newhall	0	c. T. Hargreaves, b. Meade	11
C. M'Lean, c. and b. D. S. Newhall	18	b. Meade	3
E. Kearney, b. Meade	5	b. D. S. Newhall	0
A. J. Greenfield, c. D. S. Newhall, b. C. A. Newhall	14	c. D. Newhall, b. C. Newhall	12
J. Whelan, c. Meade, b. D. S. Newhall	4	b. Meade	0
D. M. Eberts, b. Meade	3	b. Meade	8
W. B. Wells, c. Thos. Hargreaves, b. C. A. Newhall	0	b. Meade	0
G. F Hall, c. and b, D. S. Newhall	4	b. Meade	10
Dr. Spragge, run out	12	b. Meade	0
J. B. Laing, b. D. S. Newhall	0	not out	1
E. G. Powell, not out	0	b. Meade	21
C. B Brodie, c. Jos. Hargreaves (Sub.), b. D. S. Newhall	0	c. and b. D. S. Newhall	6
Byes 5, Leg bye 1, Wides 2	8	Byes 2, Leg byes 2	4
Total	68	Total	76

RUNS AT THE FALL OF EACH WICKET.

	1	2	3	4	5	6	7	8	9	10	11
PHILADELPHIA—First Innings.	10	21	28	38	39	76	92	107	111	112	117
" Second Innings.	13	55	65	98	98	98	98	113	113	114	114
CANADA—First Innings.	0	17	35	39	47	47	47	66	66	68	68
" Second Innings.	14	14	39	44	50	54	54	57	68	68	76

(OVER.)

More detailed than its English contemporaries

145

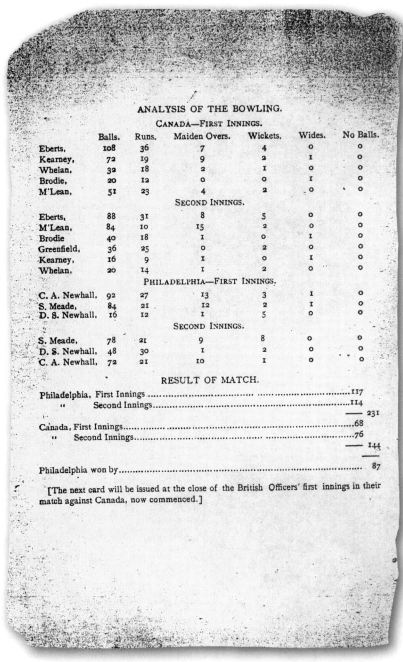

ANALYSIS OF THE BOWLING.

CANADA—FIRST INNINGS.

	Balls.	Runs.	Maiden Overs.	Wickets.	Wides.	No Balls.
Eberts,	108	36	7	4	0	0
Kearney,	72	19	9	2	1	0
Whelan,	32	18	2	1	0	0
Brodie,	20	12	0	0	1	0
M'Lean,	51	23	4	2	0	0

SECOND INNINGS.

	Balls.	Runs.	Maiden Overs.	Wickets.	Wides.	No Balls.
Eberts,	88	31	8	5	0	0
M'Lean,	84	10	15	2	0	0
Brodie	40	18	1	0	1	0
Greenfield,	36	25	0	2	0	0
Kearney,	16	9	1	0	1	0
Whelan,	20	14	1	2	0	0

PHILADELPHIA—FIRST INNINGS.

	Balls.	Runs.	Maiden Overs.	Wickets.	Wides.	No Balls.
C. A. Newhall,	92	27	13	3	1	0
S. Meade,	84	21	12	2	1	0
D. S. Newhall,	16	12	1	5	0	0

SECOND INNINGS.

	Balls.	Runs.	Maiden Overs.	Wickets.	Wides.	No Balls.
S. Meade,	78	21	9	8	0	0
D. S. Newhall,	48	30	1	2	0	0
C. A. Newhall,	72	21	10	1	0	0

RESULT OF MATCH.

Philadelphia, First Innings 117
    "   Second Innings 114
                                                —— 231

Canada, First Innings 68
    "   Second Innings 76
                                                —— 144

Philadelphia won by 87

[The next card will be issued at the close of the British Officers' first innings in their match against Canada, now commenced.]

Scorecard for Canada v Philadelphia match at Philadelphia 1875 [MCC]

146

Yorkshire scorecards of the same period have all initials before, though the amateurs are distinguished by a dagger before their names, even when as with Test Matches at Headingley, it is the whole of the visiting side.

The distinction tends to disappear in *Wisden* earlier than on scorecards: post-war editions draw no distinction: pre-war editions have 'Mr' in front of the amateurs' names. The very earliest *Wisdens* tend to have initials plus surname for the Players and Rev., Hon., Esq. or whatever, as appropriate, for the Gentlemen. 'Esq.' soon becomes 'Mr', though there is a time when the Gentlemen are 'Esq.' when they bat and 'Mr' when they bowl.

The scorecards of the London grounds continue the sharp amateur–professional divide until just before the distinction is formally abolished in 1962. With the magnanimity of those condoning the invention of the wheel, the Surrey Committee minutes for 21 March 1962 record that:

> The Chairman suggested, and it was unanimously agreed, that in future the initials of both Amateurs and Professionals should be placed before their names on the scorecards in the same way as would be done by the MCC and an asterisk would indicate those players who were amateurs. (19)

As mentioned above, Yorkshire had introduced the practice on their cards some time before, and by 1962 had in fact abandoned it, anticipating the future and giving everyone full initials before their surname with no indication as to whether they were amateurs or otherwise.

I have mentioned earlier the sluggish osmosis by which bowling figures became part of the recorded score, being first kept in MCC scorebooks in the 1840s, gradually percolating into the system and taking the remainder of the century to become universal practice, even then not always appearing in some of the public schools scorecards in *Wisden* as late as the 1960s.

The *Wisden Book of Cricket Memorabilia* suggests that cards printed in London did not carry the bowling analysis until 1893, although the same publication contains a photograph of the 1878 scorecard of MCC and Ground v Australia which does have bowling figures (It also has the scorers' names – one with an initial and one without) (20), but the custom is more honoured in the breach than the observance until the twentieth century. There was a suggestion in 1897 (21) that the bowling analysis be included on the Surrey cards, but it was not until 1903 that it was found possible to act on it.

The recording of the fall of wickets was not a regular feature until the 1890s and although the names of umpires are usually recorded, there is no general pattern to recording the names of the scorers. They are mentioned on some nineteenth-century cards and although they now appear on all first-class cards as a matter of routine, it was not until the 1970s that the practice was introduced at Surrey.

Ironically, given that England claims to have given birth to the modern game, such overseas scorecards of the nineteenth century that exist tend to be fuller. A card of California v Victoria of 1869 contains rudimentary bowling figures of wickets and runs, and those printed for the Philadelphia v Canada fixture of 1875, although not mentioning the names of umpires or scorers, do include the fall of wickets and full bowling analysis. Likewise, the card issued for a Premiership Pennant match under the aegis of the Victorian Cricket Association for the Carlton v University fixture in 1896 has fall of wickets and the full bowling analysis. Doubtless the University side wish it hadn't. The match was played on 18 January, 1, 8 and 10 February and Carlton scored 922. (22)

Purchasing a scorecard and completing the details of every wicket is, however, a particularly English habit: boards on the major grounds overseas are sufficiently detailed as to render scorecards superfluous, but, as in the Sunday League in England, they have been replaced by glossy magazine-type programmes which reflect the commercialism that is now part of the game. Few will find their way into collections, whereas to judge by the queues that form at the Printing Department at Lord's at the end of Test Matches and Cup Finals, there is still something of a vogue for collecting cards of memorable cricketing occasions.

It is doubtful whether current enthusiasm for collecting scorecards as souvenirs is in the same league as it was in 1880, when in The Oval Test Match:

> The supply of score-cards gave out towards the finish, and the spectators were seen at the printers' box presenting envelopes and leaves out of note books to ensure a copy of the official record. (23)

Cricket anthologies and pavilion walls tend to be decorated with cards recording notable events, such as MacLaren's 424, Hobbs's hundredth century, Laker's nineteen wickets, Surrey's 14 all out etc., often with a signature or two to increase interest.

But overall, other forms of communication are rendering the scorecard less significant, if not superfluous. One of the saddest entries on a card and one which is believed to be unique in first-class cricket is against the name of the 17-year-old Abdul Aziz who, playing for Karachi against the Combined Services in the Quaid-e-Azam Trophy Final, collapsed at the wicket and died on his way to hospital. The entry in the first innings is 'retired hurt 0' and in the second 'absent dead', an obituary which may soon be no less appropriate for the faithful old scorecard with its distinguished history.

Chapter Eleven

Statistics

Although scoring and statistics are close stable-mates and a club may have a scorer and statistician who is one and the same person, they are separate disciplines, scoring being concerned with the immediate record of a match and statistics with a cumulative record of a series of matches, performances of a player or team over a period, against particular opponents on a particular ground, in a particular type of cricket etc.

The distinction is not absolute, however, as each match generates its own statistics in the way of scoring rates, time, balls, fours, sixes in an individual innings etc. and, as Surrey's scorer, I frequently receive requests from the public for information on Surrey's players of the past or indeed the Test records of current Surrey players, which are not strictly speaking part of the job of the County scorer *qua* scorer. Certainly, although as indicated in Chapter Five, it is part of the job to keep the club's management up to date on career statistics of the County's players and, indeed, of the opposition's players, providing information on extra-club statistics to interested parties is the province of the statistician rather than the scorer. The line between the two, however, is blurred and there is an area of overlap.

It will be understood, therefore, that scoring is the primary discipline and statistics, though doubtless more complicated, more refined and, at times more scientific, are dependent for their existence on the information supplied by the scorers.

Just as chronologically the scoresheet precedes and informs the averages, so historically, the discipline of scoring precedes that of statistics. We saw in Chapter One how notching gradually gave way to pencil and paper methods and in Chapter Ten how scorecards were produced as a permanent record of matches. There is a possible reference in 1779 in the Order Book of the Hambledon Club to the cumulative notches of each player, but no reference to a batting average. Britcher, as indicated in Chapter One, had calculated aggregates and averages of batsmen for 1793, but it was not until 1844 when *Bell's Life* began to take an interest in such matters, that there was any attempt at more detailed statistics.

Compared to the plethora of data spawned by the contemporary game, these statistics are fairly crude and primitive and the average number of runs per innings (including not outs, which it had not yet become the practice to

deduct to arrive at the divisor) is the principal performance indicator.
Thus, we have: (1)

Batters	No. of matches	No. of innings	Greatest runs in match	Greatest runs in innings	Total runs	Avge each innings	No
Hammond	6	11	60	58	215	19.½	0
C G Taylor Esq	12	21	107	100	400	19	2
Bushby	8	15	63	54	280	18.⅔	2
Pilch	19	38	80	50	577	15.⅔	4

There is earlier evidence, however, of individual interest in the concept of a batting average. The 1834 'Club Keepers' at Eton College were Ryle and Long and there is on the back fly-leaf of the scorebook a list of figures which a little detective work soon identifies as Ryle's scores. These total 655 in 52 innings and are followed by a little piece of arithmetic:

52) 655 (12=31
624.

It seems to be a one-off: there are no calculations for any other members of the team and certainly no attempt at tabulated averages.

Simplistic and raw as they were, it should be recalled that the statistics in *Bell's Life* were ahead of anything else around in cricket at the time. It would be a further 15 years before Darwin's *Origin of Species* hit the market and the serious use of statistics in the social sciences was still half a century away. Sir Francis Galton, who formulated the concept of normal distribution and the correlation coefficient, had yet to begin his life's work; the birth of Francis Edgeworth, who was to identify statistical regularities in election results, Greek verse and the mating of bees, generalise the law of error and work on index numbers, was a year away; Karl Pearson, who was to develop notions of 'goodness of fit' at University College, London, and prepare lectures that became 'The Grammar of Science' was at his peak some 50 years later and Ronald Fisher, the father of significance tests was not born until 1890. (2) (3) So, as cricket statistics develop in the nineteenth century they do so in the context of a science that is still in its infancy and it is against that background that they should be judged rather than against their more refined and sophisticated successors a 100 years later.

Wisden made its first appearance in 1864 and only slowly did it move towards any sense of cumulative records and more than 20 years were to elapse before it began to get to grips with averages. True to the pattern of scorebooks and scorecards, it was only in 1870 that bowling figures gain any recognition. They appear under the headings of:

Overs Maidens Runs Wides No Balls Wkts

but are not, however, available in every case and Marlborough College v MCC and Ground is not the only match where something like 'Particulars of the bowling could not be obtained' is recorded. Even where they can be obtained and are included, their accuracy is perhaps questionable. For instance, F.A. Eaton Esq., playing for MCC and Ground against Hertfordshire is recorded as 'given out' and one wonders whether the scorers and/or Press might not have sought the reason for the dismissal from the umpires and duly credited one of the bowlers with another wicket.

In fairness, it must be said that Haygarth was somewhat earlier in his attempts to include bowling figures, though some of the early ones in the 1840s are fairly rudimentary, being just 'balls'. (Doubtless, the same sentiments might be expressed about subsequent, more detailed figures.) Later there are 'Balls and Runs' (so, in some cases, early economy rates are calculable); yet other matches have 'Balls Runs Wides' and, delightfully and archaically, 'Noes'.

The Editor of *Wisden* justifies the inclusion of bowling figures in the following terms:

> This year the Compiler has tried to do justice to the Bowler, by recording, wherever they were attainable, the bowling summaries to each match, thus bringing 'The Ball and the Bowler' into equally fair prominence and notice with 'The Bat and the Batsman' and thereby more equitably telling 'The Story of Cricket 1869'.

Scores and Biographies, however, does not demonstrate the same progress. As late as 1895 when Volume 14 was published, Haygarth, in the best Harrovian and MCC tradition which sees cricket as a batsman's game, still consciously omits maiden overs on the grounds that they are superfluous and is still expressing bowling figures in terms of balls, runs and wides, noting, as a matter of passing interest, that bowling figures are never preserved in the MCC books.

The inclusion of bowling figures, however rudimentary and questionable the accuracy, was nevertheless a step that verged on the revolutionary in social as well as cricketing terms. The batsmen were the amateurs and members; the bowlers, the professionals, the hired hands who appeared in *Wisden* as 'Bowlers engaged for 1869', even if their forte were batting.

x "not out"

Name	Total of runs	No. of Innings	Largest Score	Times not without scoring	Times "not out"	Average
Tremlett	424	39	38	2	1	$11\frac{3}{19}$
Reay	582	44	77	10	5	$14\frac{12}{13}$
Hoare	440	48	37	5	1	$9\frac{17}{47}$
Dupuis	486	45	101	3	1	$11\frac{1}{22}$
Hayter	276	34	28^x	3	4	$9\frac{1}{5}$
Northey	311	43	36	7	3	$7\frac{31}{40}$
Wodehouse	191	46	18^x	11	3	$4\frac{19}{43}$
Yorke	311	49	36	10	4	$6\frac{41}{45}$
Bagge	189	33	17	4	3	$6\frac{3}{10}$
Bowden	247	36	55	4	7	$8\frac{15}{29}$
S. Windham	208	38	26	8	5	$6\frac{10}{53}$

Eton College averages 1852 [by kind permission of the Provost and Fellows of Eton College] for 1852

Bowling

	No. of Wickets	No. of Innings	Greatest in Innings	Average
...lett	170	44	14	$3\frac{19}{22}$
...ay	27	11	9	$2\frac{5}{11}$
...are	144	47	7	$3\frac{3}{47}$
...orthey	98	41	6	$2\frac{16}{41}$
...agge	19	14	5	$1\frac{5}{14}$

In one way, the scorecards given in *Wisden* were more informative than they are today in that not only were substitute catchers identified, but also the fielder substituted: so whereas today's version would read simply 'c sub' or, in some versions 'c sub (Bloggs)', the 1870 version would read 'c Bloggs (for Smith)'.

At this time statistical summaries of the performances of the counties and their players were included. There was, however, no concept of national averages, though 1867 did see the first listing of 'Births and Deaths of Cricketers', and 1869 a listing of individual scores of more than 200 runs.

In 1887 'Amateur Batting Averages' and 'Amateur Bowling Averages' for first-class matches only appeared. There were then similar tables for the professionals, the whole set of statistics following those for the Parsees who toured in 1886.

The headings for the batting averages were:

Inns Runs Most in Inns Times Not Out Av'ge.

and for the bowling, the now traditional:

O M R W Av'ge

Amateurs and professionals remained distinct for a few years, both in the presentation of their averages and in every other way. The 1891 edition contained an advertisement for John Wisden's famous 'Catapulta' a bowling machine, based on the bow and arrow principle which, it was claimed, was 'invaluable to Clubs who cannot keep a professional'. Amateur and professional lists were combined into 'first-class Averages' in 1895 and have remained thus ever since.

Somewhat in advance of *Wisden* and quite probably anything else at the time, except *Bell's Life* were the scorebooks of Eton College where averages for the season were included from 1852. The batting appears under the headings 'Total of Runs', 'No of Innings', 'Largest Score', 'Times out without scoring', 'Times not out' and 'Average'. The average is still given as a vulgar fraction – e.g. 11 $\frac{3}{19}$ – but unlike *Bell's Life* eight years earlier, is calculated on the number of *completed* innings – i.e. total innings less not outs – and apart from the non-decimalisation of the fractions, these could very well be a contemporary set of batting averages.

There are also bowling averages, though the average is calculated on the number of wickets per innings and the headings are: 'No of wickets', 'No of innings', 'Greatest no in innings' and 'Average'. In a way, the logic is impeccable. The batting average is the number of runs per innings, so the bowling average is the number of wickets per innings, even when under 'Greatest no in innings', an entry of 14 betrays the fact that some matches were played against more than 11 players. Runs per wicket or even runs per over were clearly not considered, but, as Dr Johnson said of a woman's preaching and a dog walking on his hind legs, it is not done well; but you are surprised to find it done at all.

In 1861 the batting averages have become slightly less sophisticated in that they are calculated on total innings rather than completed innings and rather than fractions, simply have a number 'over'; but the bowling averages, while using the same 'number over' method, demonstrate an unprecedented degree of sophistication and are listed under 12 headings.

Innings-balls-overs-runs-maidens-wickets-average of runs per over-balls for each wicket-runs for each wicket-wides-no balls-wickets per innings.

Thus, although the concept of average wickets per innings has been maintained, we have, as well as the traditional bowling average of runs per wicket, an exceptionally early example of the strike rate (balls for each wicket) and economy rate (runs per over).

The compiler was the captain for the year, one R.A.H. Mitchell, who played for and subsequently captained Oxford University and returned to Eton as an Assistant Master. His son, Sir Frank Herbert Mitchell, was Assistant Private Secretary to King George VI.

The 'number over' method of expressing averages remained in use for some time and it was not until the 1890s that decimal fractions became the norm. Lillywhite's *Cricketers' Annual* made the switch in 1891, *Cricket* in 1893 has examples of both, and only in 1899 did *Wisden* adopt the decimal method. Before that, what appears to be a decimal point is simply a device for separating the integer and the remainder, so when in his recent biography of W.G. Grace, Simon Rae questions the great man's competence at long division when he calculates his own average for his *annus mirabilis* of 1876, he has completely missed the point that what is recorded is a 'number over', not a decimal fraction. (4)

The presentation of statistics was thus more advanced at Eton and possibly in other public schools than it was in the first-class game, but in the context of the nineteenth century, it is perhaps not surprising that it should be so – for a number of reasons. Firstly, one would expect that educational standards and levels of numeracy would be higher than elsewhere; secondly, Eton drew its clientele from the same social stratum as the MCC which was at the time the country's – indeed, the world's – premier cricket club; and thirdly, public schools cricket was of greater significance then, Eton v Harrow ranking almost as high in the summer's programme as Gentlemen v Players and Oxford v Cambridge. Nor should the different approach to statistics be considered unusual: unlike the situation obtaining elsewhere, batting and bowling figures are given equal statistical prominence, which perhaps reflects the absence of class distinction within the College XI compared with that between the College and the world outside.

Notwithstanding the above, the evidence suggests that the Harrow statistics for the same period were somewhat less sophisticated:

> The records of Harrow cricket in ancient times were not kept on any system which is known to us in the present era of statistics. But in the room which is sacred to the Philathletic Club are to be found the score-books of the Fifth and Sixth Forms. (5)

The scorebooks contain calculations of batting averages of the Sixth Form Game of around 1862–3 when I.D. Walker was captain, but apparently no tabular presentation.

It was the 1890s that saw the first statistical explosion, possibly related to the expansion in the social sciences and the need to measure things to which reference is made above. In the early part of the 1889 season *Cricket* was advertising Tufnell's *Individual Player Batting and Bowling Charts* with detailed descriptions, methods of using them, modes of publication, opinions by eminent cricketers etc. It contained specimen charts already completed for Dr W.G. Grace and others and included the following endorsement from Mr A.G. Steel: 'For people who take an interest in averages, their own or other persons', they will be invaluable.'

In the issue of 28 January 1897, the editor of *Cricket* in a feature 'Ten years of first class cricket in England' introduces the concept of the 'Figure of Merit' by adding the average runs per wicket to the average overs per wicket – an early example, though by no means as early as the Eton College one – of what is now known as the strike rate. The figures for the two leading bowlers are as follows:

	Balls	Runs	Wickets	Av'ge runs/wkt	Av'ge overs/wkt	Figure of Merit
C T B Turner	24140	8341	678	12.30	7.12	19.42
Richardson (T)	27558	13491	935	14.42	5.89	20.31

'Balls' rather than 'overs' is given because of the transition from four- to five-ball overs in 1889. The average overs per wicket is then based on the five-ball over.

There is a degree of realism about the value of statistics about which it is worth reminding ourselves 100 years later. In setting averages and statistics in the context of the game, he says:

> I am far from arguing that any averages whatever give an exact idea of a man's ability. Too great a reliance on statistics is ridiculous. But averages have this value: they give some approximate idea of the work done by a player when they are spread over a period of years, than when they merely represent the work of one year. And I honestly believe that the system I have used in the averages which follow is a truer, if slightly more cumbrous test, than the ordinary system.

The distinction was and remains an important one and it is axiomatic that a Test batting average of 40 or a bowling average of 20 over a decade are of more significance than the same figures in the first-class averages after half a season when fixtures may have included a couple of matches against the universities.

The statistical spawn continued and *Cricket* was becoming more statistics orientated: in the same issue, F.S. Ashley-Cooper, successor to Arthur Haygarth as doyen of biographers and statisticians, has a lengthy feature on the batting career of W.G. Grace, including *inter alia* how Dr Grace has been dismissed while playing for Gloucestershire 1868-96; grounds on which Dr Grace has scored his runs for Gloucestershire: Dr Grace's batting averages for MCC 1869–96; a table showing against which clubs Dr Grace has scored his runs for MCC; how Dr Grace has been dismissed while playing for MCC; his batting average in North v South matches 1866–96; names of the bowlers by whom Dr Grace has been bowled and of the fielders by whom he has been caught. There is no suggestion that the information might serve any useful purpose: it is sheer statistics for the sake of statistics, a self-indulgent extravaganza and fascinating for the minority to which it appeals.

The statistical revolution was now in full swing: in the eighteenth century there was not much need for statistics, except to indicate the results of matches for gambling purposes, but now there was an attempt at the statistical measurement of individual performance and just as the statistics of, for instance, the Census of Population become more detailed, so do those which measure the sporting and economic activities of that population.

Crude averages, as we have seen were published first by Britcher in 1790 and later by *Bell's Life* in 1844. *The Times* did not give full scores of matches until 1848, but as statistics develop alongside and as an integral part of economics and other social sciences, so cricket statistics become simultaneously both more extensive and more detailed, so that by 1903 we have lists of heavy defeats, large partnerships, innings of 400 + alongside comparisons of runs per wicket on each Test ground in England and Australia.

Only in the order of the columns did *Wisden*'s presentation of statistics change much before the 1980s when there were further additions and refinements. In 1982, columns for 100s and best bowling were added to the batting and bowling averages respectively and in 1986, a column for matches played was added to the batting. In 1988, catches and stumpings were added to the batting figures and five-wicket innings to the bowling. The catches and stumpings disappeared in the following year to be replaced by 50s. A separate section on fielding was introduced with a qualification of 20 dismissals

The ABC's *Australian Cricket Almanack* and Allan's *Australian Cricket Annual*, Antipodean equivalents of *Wisden* have statistics of a more detailed nature. For instance, first-class scorecards include minutes, balls, fours and sixes for each batsman and statistical summaries have, where appropriate, scoring rate (runs per 100 balls), strike rate (balls per wicket) and economy rate (runs conceded per over).

The advent of the computer and the ease with which statistics can be generated has, in cricket and other areas of life, produced all kinds of data previously inconceivable and with it the temptation of generating and disseminating information merely because it is capable of being generated and disseminated. Paralysis by analysis rules, calling for discernment between what Mike Ringham calls 'orthodox' and 'statistical overload'.

Supplying the former, though it is more than capable of feeding the latter also, is Gordon Vince's Cricket Statistics System used by a number of statisticians, county scorers and Sky Sports. Using a unique number for every player, this has on it scorecards for every Limited Overs International, every Test match and all first-class matches from 1989. It will soon include all English domestic limited overs cricket. Ultimately, the aim is to load on to the database details of every first-class match ever played (presumably a few megabytes of disk space will be required) from which point it will be possible to generate an even greater variety of interrelated statistics than it does at the moment. It is capable of being used to maintain player and match details and generate a range of averages and statistics. Mike Ringham has a not dissimilar but less ambitious system, Australian Cricket Programmes, limited to club cricket and aimed at producing data for selectors, coaches, captains and the annual report.

The Vince database has its origins in, and is also used to generate, the information for the sophisticated Coopers and Lybrand ratings, which take into account not only the raw data of runs scored and wickets taken, but also the strength of the opposition and the state of the match (not the state of the pitch as that is not for this purpose statistically measurable). Most recent form is more heavily weighted, the latest performance being weighted at 100 per cent, the previous one at 96 per cent and so on on a sliding scale. Originally launched in 1987 by Deloittes as the equivalent of golf's Sony ratings, they were the brainchild of Ted Dexter, are published monthly in *The Cricketer International* and are paralleled in county cricket by the Whyte and Mackay rankings in which the players take an interest, because there is prize money riding on the final tables.

There are other pieces of data, some more interesting than others and some which have far more to do with statistics than with cricket. Recently, for example, there has been information presented in the form of a brightly coloured histogram, on LBW decisions in Test matches for and against the host country and average runs scored at each position in the batting order. (6) We are close to the area of lies, damned lies and statistics as the data purports to demonstrate 'home bias' in India, Pakistan and Sri Lanka and that England have a weakness at no 3 and no 6. While it is true that statistics never tell you nothing, it is also true that they rarely tell you everything and in the cases mentioned are of limited value, unless it is known whether the LBW decisions in question were good or bad ones and who occupied the no 3 and no 6 berths.

A more recent example of statistics for the sake of statistics is Sky Sports 'catches per match', surely virtually meaningless unless it is accompanied by information on the number of chances offered. An approach based on statistics alone, where statistical relationships become an end in themselves and make no pretence of providing a service to the game, can be fallacious and misleading, such as attempts to apply actuarial techniques and life expectancy tables to batting averages and predict the score at which a batsman is likely to be dismissed (7) as in an article I read recently which purported to demonstrate that a batsman was more vulnerable at certain scores. Like attempts to forecast football results on the basis of statistical trends, it fails to take account of human fallibility and inconsistency; for example, whether a batsman gets out at a particular score is less dependent on the number showing against him on the scoreboard than on whether the next ball is a long-hop or in-swinging yorker.

Like a self-perpetuating bureaucracy, statistics may become an end in themselves rather than a means to an end and self-serving, rather than cricket-serving. An example of what I mean was contained in an item on the Agenda for the 1997 AGM of the Association of Cricket Statisticians which suggested that a wide ball should count as a ball faced by the batsman. In statistical terms it should because it is delivered and faced and a batsman can be out from it; but in cricketing terms, the purpose of recording balls received is to measure speed of scoring (albeit with the recognition that it is a crude indicator, given that it tells us nothing about the kind of ball that has been received) and it is logical that wides should be excluded since, by definition, no runs to the batsman can accrue from them. I remain unconvinced by the argument that they should be included because a batsman can be out from them, since the likelihood of being stumped or hit wicket from a wide is well below that of being run out from a ball he does not receive.

The thoroughness and refinement of cricket statistics is very much a post-Second World War phenomenon. Though pre-war match reports were more detailed in the way of describing what went on and sometimes more accurate than the official version on the statistics of a particular game, they were not as succinct on setting the details in a historical context as their successors. When Michael Atherton carried his bat through a completed Test innings at Christchurch in February 1997, Sky Sports immediately conveyed the information that this was the eighth occasion it had been done for England and that Atherton was the seventh batsman to do it. Most of the Press carried the information the following day. By contrast when Percy Fender scored what was at the time the world's fastest first-class century in 1920, few of the Press seemed to appreciate that it was a record though a few had a vague, unspecified feeling that it might be.

Two years ago there was a mildly acrimonious dispute between the Association of Cricket Statisticians and the Editor of *Wisden* on the accuracy of the Almanack, the former claiming that the latter was full of errors and that about 70 per cent of its scorecards were inaccurate. The debate was summed up as follows by a *Times* leader on (and the date may have at least a partial significance) 1 April 1995:

> Cricket has few features more compelling than the rich pedantry of its statistics. *Wisden*, treasured even by many who have never played the game, is proof of this. Yet cricket-lovers are nothing if not disputatious spirits. Members of the Association of Cricket Statisticians and Historians, described by sceptics as the cricketing equivalent of train-spotters in anoraks, have uncovered a degree of statistical inaccuracy in editions before 1970, which they set at about 70% of all *Wisden* scorecards. One can almost hear the glug of slashed wrists as the game's faithful respond in the manner of betrayed lovers.

There was some debate on the meaning of 'inaccurate' and whether a bye recorded as a leg bye rendered a whole card inaccurate, but the final word lay with Matthew Engel, the Editor, who, clearly aware of the unsound judgements that result from applying contemporary conventions and standards to historical documents, dismissed the debate in a couple of sentences: 'The science of cricket statistics was not always at the level of sophistication it is now. It was simply not that important. (8)

And certainly the concern with accuracy, like that with records and thoroughness,is a relatively new phenomenon. Just as for music lovers, the pleasure of an orchestral concert lies in the sound created and not in the score from which it is played, so for most cricket players and followers, the essence of the game is the contest between bat and ball with the best matches a coalescence of runs, wickets and time. Yes, the result is important and individual achievement is important, but the method by which that achievement is measured within a match is of secondary importance and its measurement across a number of matches of very limited significance.

Nevertheless, to a small but dedicated band, epitomised in the Association of Cricket Statisticians and (a recent appendage) Historians, the accuracy of cricket records takes on an almost religious significance. There was for a brief period immediately after the Second World War a Society of Cricket Statisticians the primary object of which was 'to prepare and publish the records of first-class cricketers', since there were inconsistencies between different publications and in the interpretation of what constituted a first-class match, particularly overseas. One of its early presidents was Hubert Preston, Editor of *Wisden* at the time.

By 1948, the Society had expanded its horizons and become The Cricket Society, though the statisticians remained a discrete group within it. It was in 1973 that the Association of Cricket Statisticians emerged as a separate and autonomous institution, though there was for a time a loose association with The Cricket Society and there was and remains some overlap of membership.

In the same way as the masons trace their ancestry to King Solomon, so the ACS, albeit less secretively, trace theirs to Arthur Haygarth (1825–1903) whose lifetime's research was the records and biographies of famous cricketers, and F.S. Ashley-Cooper who continued his work. The Association has done sterling work in producing records of early matches which are as accurate as ever likely to be achieved. Absolute accuracy is unachievable. It has already been mentioned in Chapter Three that many county scorebooks are missing and even where they have survived, cannot inevitably be regarded as an infallible primary source. The real primary source is what actually happened on the field and if that is incorrectly recorded, then the error is likely to be compounded.

In an article on the Surrey Statistics Group, a mini-version of the ACS, but one with similar objectives, Michael Pearce tells how he tracked down the accurate version of the dismissal of Yorkshire's J. Rowbotham against Surrey at Sheffield in 1866. The versions were c Griffith b Southerton (Surrey scorebook, Yorkshire scorebook and *Wisden*), c Noble b Griffith (*Scores and Biographies*) and c Griffith b Noble (*Sheffield Daily Telegraph*). (9) In the context of eternity, it did not matter too much, but it is illustrative of the lengths to which the statistician will go and the number of sources to be consulted to arrive at the most likely of the various versions of events.

Likewise, amid esoteric offerings on *Umpires in Non-Championship First-Class Matches since 1900* and *Minor Counties against the Tourists,* (10) the Association has produced reputable publications on what constitutes a first-class match, statistical Wisden-style surveys from 1864 to 1872, annuals for minor counties and first-class counties 2nd XIs as well as booklets on county grounds, cricketers from various counties and states and a 'Famous Cricketers' series which records every innings and every wicket taken by its subjects. Most significantly, however, it has produced scorecards which, given that there are bound to be some uncertainties which can never be resolved, are as accurate as it is possible to be on the scores of all first class matches played in the nineteenth century. With its more scientific and professional approach, the Association is on the way to replacing *Wisden* as the authority on the game's records and statistics.

Cricket has been represented on the Internet since 1993 and it is perhaps a refection on the popularity of the game – at least in attracting arm's length followers, if not necessarily regular spectators – that Cricinfo is the second most popular sports Web-site after the United States NBA. (11) Whether or not cricket is a better or more popular game than it was when Britcher produced his aggregates and averages in 1793 or young Ryle calculated his batting average in the back of the Eton scorebook of 1836, its statistics are certainly more sophisticated and more immediately accessible to a wider spectrum of enthusiasts.

Chapter Twelve

Politics and Administration

It is perhaps symptomatic of the way cricket scoring has been media-led and reactive rather than self-motivated and pro-active that in the decade after Thatcherism had succeeded in diluting the power of organised labour, the Association of County Cricket Scorers should emerge. It is not a trade union, indeed it has taken a deliberate and conscious decision not to become one and, although like any organisation, some of its members may be more militant than others, it traces its roots not to strongly held Marxist and Leninist views emanting from shipyards or coalmines, but to an annual informal luncheon, initiated by county 2nd XI scorers at a hostelry conveniently adjacent to the railway station in Derby.

The cradle was thus in place for the Association to be born at the Midland Hotel on 17 November 1993, catalysed by a common grievance about the imposition with minimal consulation and training of a highly imperfect computerised scoring system, but also by an alleged positive desire to improve standards of scoring and to establish a point of contact with the TCCB, such as that enjoyed by the Professional Cricketers' Association and the First Class Umpires Association. Ted Lester, Yorkshire's scorer from 1962 to 1992 was elected the first Chairman. The original objects of the Association were innocuous and uncontentious enough and were as follows:

to improve the standards of cricket scoring;
to promote, improve, protect and uphold the status of County Cricket scorers both individually and collectively;
to co-operate and cultivate good relations with all bodies associated with cricket for the betterment of the game;
to take such action and make such recommendations as may be considered desirable in the interests of cricket and necessary for the benefit of scorers in particular;
to promote the social affairs of the membership.

The Association had its own magazine, *The Scorer*, edited by Michael

Ayers, former Surrey scorer, which attracts contributions on scoring and related matters from all areas of the game. The cover of the first issue was adorned by a reproduction of Thomas Henwood's well-known 1842 lithograph which bears the same name as the fledgling magazine and which is probably the earliest known representation of a scorer (as opposed to a notcher). The sitter was William Davies, scorer to Lewes Priory and Sussex County Cricket Club; claret glass and bottle at his left elbow and a second, empty bottle on the ground. Unlikely to be the ancestor of Bill (Lancashire) or Alex (Warwickshire) who spells his 'Davis' differently anyway, he is the icon and role model for scorers in a more leisurely age. *The Scorer* has after 17 issues been succeeded by a more informal newsletter.

Scorers are in general a mild-mannered group of men (and they are all men at the moment, though there are a couple of women on the reserve list), partly, I suppose, because the nature of the job attracts that kind of person, the long-serving member or ex-player so in love with the game that they are prepared to spend whole summers in its service, including weeks away from home and consider it a privilege to be paid (however little) for something they enjoy. And it is perhaps because there has always been a ready supply of such people that the economic laws of supply and demand have operated and pay has remained low.

But the scene is changing; the uneasy co-existence of the professional and the amateur, culminating in the abolition of the distinction in 1962 has been referred to earlier in the book. The scorebox is now catching up. Attendances at first-class cricket are declining (though Test Matches and limited-overs competitions tell a different story) and former professional cricketers, as well as being better remunerated during their playing days, have more post-retirement opportunities for coaching, marketing and media work.

Although county scorers, most of whom would admit to being fairly low on a scale of computer literacy, have adapted well to the computer revolution in the scorebox, many would confess to enjoying the job less than they used to and to being attracted by retirement (a second retirement in some cases). They are being gradually replaced by younger, computer-literate men like Keith Gerrish of Gloucestershire, Brian Hunt of Durham, John Potter of Yorkshire, Gordon Stringfellow of Nottinghamshire and Tony Kingston of Northamptonshire, career scorers in the same mould as Hampshire's Vic Isaacs, Statistician of the Year for 1996, and though still relatively young, the longest-serving scorer on the county circuit.

At several points in this study I have commented on the accuracy of some early scorebooks and the absence of care demonstrated by most county clubs in the preservation of their books of primary record. Gerald Brodribb, who preceded the ACS in undertaking a study of county scorebooks, remarks on the amateurishness, untidiness and faulty arithmetic of some of the early ones and the improvement witnessed over the last 30 years. (1) We are, I think, just about at a point where the transition from amateurism to professionalism is on the way to completion and likely to be reflected in pay and conditions. Since 1979, thanks to the Professional Cricketers' Association, there has been a minimum salary for capped players and a considerable improvement in remuneration. Pay for umpires has also been standardised (one area where the ethos of 'payment by results' has not yet penetrated). As far as scorers are concerned, although fees for Test Matches and Limited Overs Internationals are determined by the ECB, rates of pay are otherwise regarded as a matter for each county. As the input and output of Cricket Record results in scorers' work becoming almost standardised, it may well be that minimum, standardised rates will be established.

In practice, however, the industrial muscle of the Association is somewhere between nil and negligible and at least three members have resigned from the ranks and others declined to join because of the alleged pusillanimity of the organisation. Had the ACCS been able to exert any influence, the TCCB would hardly have recruited a scorer from outside the county circuit to accompany England on the last four winter tours (South Africa and the World Cup in 1995–96, Zimbabwe and New Zealand in 1996–97 and Sharjah, the West Indies in 1997–98 and Australia in 1998–99). The England scorer on the two previous tours (West Indies in early 1994 and Australia in 1994–95) had been Alex Davis of Warwickshire and before that the berth had been occupied by Clem Driver of Essex.

There was no suggestion that either of them had not been up to the job, nor failed to live up to the high standards of scoring to which the ACCS would wish to aspire, but when Ray Illingworth, the England team manager, wished to have Malcolm Ashton, with whom he had worked on BBC Television, as his scorer in South Africa and in India and Pakistan for the World Cup, the TCCB acceded to his wishes. Some scorers were at the time in favour of vigorous protest, but the nearest to any industial action was an acrimonious exhange of correspondence between the Cricket Secretary of TCCB, the Chairman of ACCS and a few individual members.

Writing in *The Scorer*, Ted Lester referred to the appointment as 'a gross and inexcusable slur on the ability and competence of all county scorers, and the manner in which the appointment was made without any form of consultation, explanation or forewarning was ill conceived, or should I say "Illy-conceived"?' (2) A year later, Illingworth was no longer team manager; the TCCB invited applications for the post, but stressed that the field would not be restricted to those 'on the circuit'. This time there was consultation with the Chairman of ACCS. Malcolm Ashton was reappointed. There were no strikes, no walk-outs, no working-to-rule.

No one is questioning the right of the game's Governing Body to appoint whomsoever they wish as scorer; nothing obliges them to limit themselves to the county circuit any more than they are obliged to pick the physiotherapist or indeed the England team from the county circuit (though a few decades have passed since they ventured outside it) and no one is suggesting that Ashton is anything other than a competent scorer, but the negotiating muscle of the ACCS was clearly not a factor which influenced the Board's decisions.

It may even be eventually that scorers will, as umpires are, be employed centrally, allocated to various matches and background statistics provided centrally. The cosy link between scorer and manager would thus be broken, and it may not happen, but it is not impossible to contemplate. After all, the employment of a limited number of international players by the ECB rather than counties has been mooted, and it was in 1882 that Yorkshire proposed to MCC that umpires be appointed for the match and not for one side or the other. (3)

The notion of a profession implies an element of exclusivity and in numerical terms, the ACCS is certainly that, the inner cabinet of a potential thirty-six members, four fewer than the Académie Française, being restricted to the 1st and 2nd XI scorers of the first-class counties, though there is a whole array of life members, associate members and friends. However, as well as exclusivity, the notion of a profession also implies training and qualifications, and those elements are absent.

To find those one has to look outside the ACCS to the much larger Association of Cricket Umpires and Scorers, an organisation dating from 1953, 10 per cent of the 6,500 members of which are scorers – who have been in its title since 1994. In truth, it is a small enough proportion , given the amount of cricket played. On the not unrealistic assumption that there is no spare capacity in the umpiring section and that most don the white coat for most summer weekends, given that the normal complement of officials is two umpires and two scorers, it follows that well over 90 per cent of cricket played in the UK is recorded by scorers who are not members of the appropriate professional body.

Formerly part of the NCA, the ACU & S prides itself on covering the 99.8 per cent of cricket that is played outside the first-class arena, still quaintly dubbed by the ECB, the 'recreational' game. At Sunday 3rd XI level in the home counties, recreational it may be; at Saturday 1st XI level in some of the northern leagues, 'recreational' is not the first epithet that springs to mind.

Be that as it may, it is the other 0.2 per cent in which most followers are interested and which attracts sponsorship and media coverage. It is quite possible to become a scorer on the county circuit without ever having heard of the ACU & S, let alone having seen an examination paper, just as it is possible to feature on the first-class umpires list or even the Test list and be, at least in ACU & S terms, unqualified. Umpires and scorers on the first-class circuit, not holding the relevant piece of paper, do not in any sense have an inferiority complex, preferring to see themselves as 'qualified by experience'.

Now that the glass ceiling between first-class cricket and the rest has been removed, is it to be assumed that the two professional bodies will begin to speak to each other? They are at the moment quite separate, and although some ACCS members are also members of and indeed office-holders in ACU & S, there has been no organised attempt on the part of the latter to involve itself in the first-class game.

There is in theory no reason why ACU & S examinations should not apply to scorers on the first-class circuit, but they would require radical revision before they could begin to be considered appropriate. There are at the moment three levels: introductory for youngsters and novices still strangers to the mysterious art; standard for the average club scorer; and so-called advanced which, as mentioned in Chapter Three, is concerned largely with linear scoring techniques and transposition between that and traditional scoring – though, rather like the three-point turn in the driving test, the occasions one would wish to do so are few and far between. I do it twice a year, transposing my linear record of the Limited Overs International and Test Match played at the Foster's Oval to the official England scorebook which has the traditional debit and credit layout. Most scorers, I suspect, have no reason to do it at all. There is nothing in the examinations on computerised scoring.

But, again like the driving test which was devised when road conditions were quite different, a test that has since been updated to reflect modern conditions, there is a case for updating these examinations which are based on scoring an innings from a written description. Surely the examination should, as far as possible, replicate reality and given that video technology has hit the scene since these examinations were first devised, it should surely not be beyond the wit of the examiners to get hold of a video of a limited overs match which involves a change of innings, a few runs, a few wickets, a few extras, run outs and the odd idiosyncrasy such as five leg byes on to the helmet or a stumping from a wide. There is an opportunity for the ACU & S to join forces with the ACCS and perhaps get just a little nearer to reality.

We have seen in earlier chapters that the quality of scoring has not always been of the highest and that there have been and continue to be various errors and uncertainties in official records, some of which, because there is no means of re-creating the match, will never be discovered, let alone, corrected. But, certainly at first-class level there is a case for improving the standards of scoring world-wide.

Theo Braganza, Secretary of the Association of Cricket Statisticians and Scorers of India (Motto: Aim for Accuracy), is an advocate of greater recognition of scorers and wishes to see their names automatically included in the record of the match, (4) alongside the increasing army of other officials, which, as well as the two umpires, can now include a Match referee, Man of the Match Adjudicator and TV Replay Umpire. While it is true, not only in India, but world-wide that recognition has been slow, there is still a way to go before the full professionalisation of scoring even at first-class level. It has lagged behind the professionalisation of playing, umpiring, training, physiotherapy and groundsmanship and there is still some way to travel when a review of the *Pepsi Cricontrol Statistical Annual 1995/96* published by the Board of Control for Cricket in India can contain the following:

> One feels that full scorecards, with modern additions such as second innings batting and bowling position, and close-of-play scores are vital, and Menon [the Editor] gives us the lot. Here he is absolutely beyond criticism and also deserves the highest possible praise for his criticisms of those associations failing to supply official scoresheets, or which allocates [sic] scorers of such mind blowing incompetence that they have to be ignored. In his editorial, Menon mentions first-class match scores which are incomplete or do not tally or which rely on various players to take turns at keeping the match details recorded. One hopes that his pleas are noted (not that an Englishman can feel superior here; despite the apparent evidence of the official scorebook, all the details of the English national partnership for a certain wicket are incorrect, due in part to the fact that one scorer allowed his wife to take over for a while. The other scorer? One would love to know what he was about). So the scoring needs bringing up to standard. (5)

In a similar vein, David Frith in the inaugural edition of *The Scorer* bewails the poor standards of scoring in the 1993 West Indies v Pakistan limited overs series and the 'rebel' tours of South Africa by Kim Hughes' Australians and regrets that much of the detail is based on *ex post facto* construction often amounting to little more than guesswork. (6)

More recently, in the 1996 World Cup, when eventual winners Sri Lanka amassed 398-5 in 50 overs against Kenya at Kandy, the scorers clearly lost their way and the corrected bowling figures, published in the Press next day but one, bore but a passing resemblance to the originals. Eight bowlers were used, including two Odumbes and two Tikolos, so the errors are understandable, but while such mistakes are being made, the claims for first-class cricket scoring to be recognised as a profession are considerably weakened. It may well be, therefore, in the light of the amount of international cricket being played these days and the relative ease with which cricketers can play in the domestic competitions of other countries, that the ACCS should be less insular and without in any way being over-complacent about standards at home, seek to improve standards overseas. It would help, of course, if the ECB as a member of the ICC could demonstrate its commitment to improving standards internationally by appointing official scorers for both senior and junior tours.

In the unaugural issue of *The Scorer*, Jack Bannister is supportive of attempts at professionalisation and writes:

> The only surprise about the formation of a county scorers' representative body is that it has taken so long to happen. The game tends to ignore those who stay quiet and the working conditions and pay of eighteen of the most important men in first-class cricket need standardising and improving.

> They said it could not happen with cricketers, but as Secretary of the Cricketers' Association for twenty years, I can tell county scorers that it can. You don't have to be militant or obstructive. Not if you have a cast-iron case which you undoubtedly do now... The job of a county scorer now calls for skills and talents far beyond those beloved qualities of the men of my time.

> If the authorities want the benefit of an ultra-modern approach, they must pay for it and good luck to the newly-formed body of scorers. (7)

That good luck was needed in 1997, however, when the worm finally turned and the ACCS threatened the first strike of scorers in more than a century of county cricket. The publicity was widespread and unprecedented. The basic reasons were twofold – the reappointment of Malcolm Ashton and the manner in which it was announced.

Ashton's second appointment, as already mentioned, was made after applications had been invited from county scorers albeit with the proviso that consideration would not be confined to those on the county circuit; it was stressed that the appointment was for 1996–97 only and would be reviewed for 1997–98.

However, for the trips to Sharjah and the West Indies in 1997–98, even that charade was side-stepped with the reappointment of Malcolm Ashton. The review promised by TCCB the previous year had been superficial and cosmetic, comprising an appraisal of Ashton's own undoubtedly competent performance, but ignoring the potential of other possible candidates, and coupled with the nature of the announcement of Ashton's reappointment (in the ECB News section of a Sunday League programme, preceded by a telephone call to the Chairman of the Association of County Cricket Scorers) spurred a number of ACCS members into action.

Several scorers wrote to John Carr, the ECB's Director of Cricket Operations. My own missive expressed dismay at the reappointment and manner of announcement. Clearly the Board could appoint whomsoever it wished in whatsoever manner it chose and could publicise the appointment by any method it chose. That much was not in question. It had no obligation to be bound by precedent and its right to move the goalposts with minimal consultation – even none – was not an issue, but its sensitivity surely, as was an answer to the question of when county scorers were to be rewarded for their efforts in getting to grips with Cricket Record, Duckworth–Lewis et al. with something other than a kick in the teeth.

John's reply was the essence of courtesy and diplomacy, pointing out that the appointment had been made by EMAC (England Management Advisory Committee) which had an obligation to appoint the scorer and the physiotherapist who it thought would perform the best task on tour, irrespective of whether they had links with any county. He was sure that Tim Lamb would have made EMAC aware of the sensitivities of the appointment. A number of scorers to whom I spoke were equally sure that neither the Chief Executive of ECB nor EMAC gave a damn about the sensitivities of county scorers.

The time had come for action; nine of the first ten scorers to whom I spoke had little hesitation about the need for an Extraordinary General Meeting of the ACCS. The requisition was sent to the Association Secretary and the meeting called for the usual central venue of Derby on Monday, 28 July. So that the meeting would have a focus for its debate, I produced a draft resolution suggesting a withdrawal of labour at all Axa Life League matches on Sunday, 31 August, a day when there was a full programme, when Duckworth–Lewis might operate and when a number of matches taking place might affect the destination of the title.

The row brewed up and for a few days the scoring communiity enjoyed rare publicity as the national and international Press and radio and television channels scented a news item. 'Scoreboard serfs ready for rebellion' screamed *The Guardian* and went on to refer to the Lackeys' Uprising or Flunkeys' rebellion. (8) A *Daily Telegraph* leader opined:

> Talk of a strike amounts to a sensation, for nothing like this has happened in the
> 130 years of county cricket. What they seek is a sympathetic ear and a degree
> more consideration. It should be accorded to them. (9)

The 1998 edition of *Wisden* in its Miscellaneous section had a couple of pages on Labour Relations and paired the scorers' flirtation with industrial action with the Australian Cricketers' Association's strike threat. Paul Weaver was as sympathetic as he had earlier been in *The Guardian*:

> The scorers are the surviving gofers of the game … underpaid and overworked, [they] are traditionally exploited by their counties. They are no fools. Anybody who can embrace the new technology and engage in hand-to-hand combat with the Duckworth/Lewis method (a scoring system the umpires took one look at and ran away from) and emerged scarred but triumphant must be respected. (10)

Tim Lamb was stirred into action and telephoned me during a break in play in Surrey's Championship match against Hampshire at Guildford. As the rain swept through the tent that was our makeshift scoring facility, he regretted the breakdown in communications that appeared to have occurred and we were, I think, both prepared to concede that these could have been better, both between ECB and ACCS and within each organisation.

He then went on to make a number of points, none of which was without validity, but to each of which a counter-argument was readily available. The England scoring appointment, he said, was not a perk, not a reward for long service or loyalty, but part of the increased professionalism of the game and there were a number of county scorers who would not be able to do it. Malcolm Ashton's performance had received glowing reports and EMAC had no hesitation about renewing the appointment after considering those reports. Administrative duties other than those associated with scoring were involved and scorers would look ridiculous if they went on strike.

I could not agree more that it was not a perk; especially in the West Indies with inter-island travel between primitive airports, it was likely to be damned hard work. If increased professionalism were required, who better to provide it than the professional body comprising and representing county scorers? Certainly there are those who could not do the job, those who would not wish to and those who would be debarred on health grounds. On the other hand, there were a number who could and who would willingly make themselves available. The quarrel is not with Malcolm Ashton personally: he is a sociable fellow, a good scorer, popular with the players and an excellent administrator. So was Alex Davis. All county scorers undertake administrative duties from custodianship of the flag upwards and a number have controlled budgets larger and more complex than those associated with an England overseas cricket tour. Scorers might look ridiculous if they went on strike: they would demonstrate that they were a totally ineffective body if they did nothing.

At the end of a lengthy conversation, punctuated by my attempts to keep in place a large sheet of polythene which was struggling to keep the driving rain from the computer, we agreed to differ and I agreed to convey Tim's points to the EGM.

Given that there were a number of 2nd XI fixtures on the appointed day and that a number of scorers were travelling between fixtures on routes not exactly adjacent to Derby, the attendance was reasonable. The mood was calm, the standard of debate high and there was an absence of hysteria and emotional outpourings. Members recalled the chequered history of the England overseas appointment from the time Fergie combined it with the post of baggage master, through the time when it was unpaid, to times when the captain was overruled by the manager to times when the manager was overruled by the captain, through to Clem Driver, Alex Davis and Malcolm Ashton. Some, with the wisdom of hindsight, felt that stronger action two years earlier might have been preferable.

Having reviewed the present position, the meeting took the view that strike action was inappropriate, especially as it would not receive 100 per cent backing from the membership or those who had lent their support to the cause – the media, players, umpires, administrators, members and the cricketing public generally. Ironically, a strike on 31 August would have been totally ineffective. Virtually the whole programme was washed out and media coverage would have been close to zero, as the day was completely overshadowed by the tragic death of Diana, Princess of Wales.

Other forms of action were considered. Doing nothing was not an option; well, it was, but the inevitable consequence was that the ACCS would revert to being a luncheon club and cease to be taken seriously as a professional body. Some consideration was given to partial strike action, namely 'pulling the plug' on Cricket Record, thereby making a point, but also continuing to provide a service. This was eventually opposed, however, on the ground that it would be hitting at the wrong target. The quarrel was not, on this occasion, with the Press Association.

Eventually a compromise, albeit a positive one, was reached whereby members agreed to try and persuade the ECB to meet them on the shared playing field of a common professional approach. The ECB through its Chief Executive had pointed to its alleged professionalism and yet for overseas 'A' tours was prepared to accept the efforts of any local scorer that might be available. If they really believed that no county scorer was worthy of consideration for the senior tour – and all the signs appeared to point that way – let them use 'A' tours in the same way as they are intended to be used for players, namely as apprenticeships to train and equip them for the more onerous responsibilities of full England tours.

In the past the Board had argued that finances did not permit scorers to be appointed for 'A' tours. That is at least questionable. The game is awash with media and sponsorship money. Let anyone who subscribes to the poverty plea have a look at the number of ECB blazers who were knocking back the rum punches in Barbados and Antigua the following March.

The eventual resolution is included at Appendix C. It was agreed to send it with a press release, a letter to all county chairmen urging them to communicate with their scorers, so that they might be fully appraised of their views when scoring matters were on the Agenda of ECB meetings, and a letter to the ECB Chairman and Chief Executive accompanying the resolution and suggesting that relationships could be improved by regular meetings of the ECB and ACCS.

The response to the Resolution was not immediate, ECB officials being involved in the self-evidently more important task of *Raising the Standard* in the form of the MacLaurin Report (although apropos of raised professionalism etc., let it be noted that the ACCS was not amomg the myriad bodies consulted!). The jury will be out for some time on whether they succeeded in doing so and although it is not too difficult to predict the verdict, it is outside the scope of this study and introduced here simply to indicate what was going on at the same time.

The Chief Executive of the ECB, while pleased about the resolution not to go ahead with industrial action, was somewhat less than delighted with the vocabulary used by what purported to be a professional association and particularly objected to the accusation of duplicity. A review had taken place and the Association had been informed of Ashton's appointment before it had been made public. Previous contempt had been disguised by a veneer of courtesy, but even that was now absent, as members were invited to agree that a review comprising the performance of the present incumbent and an *ex post facto* telephone call had fulfilled earlier commitments and were the maximum they were entitled to expect. There was no justification for not renewing the engagement and no point in making a change for changes's sake. It seemed to have been forgotten that the Association had used similar arguments two years earlier when Alex Davis was deposed in favour of Malcolm Ashton.

The response to the proposal that scorers should accompany 'A' and Under 19 tours was at most lukewarm. It would be considered, but no other ICC member did it, so why should we? I was reminded of F.M. Cornford's dictum in *Microcosmographia Academica* that for fear of creating a dangerous precedent, nothing should ever be done for the first time. The costs argument was rolled out again and accompanied by an additional argument that there had been no difficulties in finding local scorers who were competent, enthusiastic and reliable.

Those qualities, however, have not invariably been reflected in the scorebooks and neither Bill Frindall nor *Wisden*'s correspondents would agree that the use of local scorers has been trouble-free. The scorebooks apparently have not shown too much improvement since the Cricketer's Bible commented on the MCC Under-25 tour of Pakistan in 1967:

> To judge from the official MCC score book returned to Lord's, some difficulty was experienced in finding competent scorers. In many instances the figures, including individual batting scores did not tally. Something better than this must be expected in the future. (11)

As recently as 1996, there is a reference to umpires having to correct scorers on a fairly obvious point of cricket law. (12)

Nor has the Board's confidence in the ability of local scorers been vindicated by events on the 1997–98 tour of Kenya and Sri Lanka. Without being unduly immodest and with all due respect to the local scorers, it is difficult to imagine that a competent county scorer conversant with playing conditions would have been party to the farce which declared England 'A' the winners in a rain-affected Limited Overs International in Nairobi, which should have been awarded to Kenya, and then a week later was declared no result.

Lamb's letter concluded with an agreement to the request for periodic meetings between officers of the ECB and ACCS, so although relations are strained, they are not completely severed.

One paradoxical effect of the Association's militant stirrings is that it has emerged not stronger, but constitutionally weaker. The strike threat prompted into action the Certification Officer for Trade Unions and Employers' Associations who saw the ACCS as an organisation whose principal purposes include the regulation of relations between workers and employees and put pressure on the Chairman and Committee to register as a trade union.

The Committee thus had the options of complying or of remaining a voluntary professional association whose rules were consonant with those of a trade union. In the event it chose neither. Without consulting members about what would have been a major constitutional change, it decided to expunge two of its rules so that there was no chance of its being regarded as a union.

It was a stance which was irrational, but one which the membership nevertheless endorsed at the 1997 Annual General Meeting by re-electing the whole committee *en bloc* and providing the two-thirds majority required for a rule change. The extinct objects are:

To promote, improve, protect and uphold the status of County Cricket Scorers both individually and collectively.

To take such action and make such recommendations as may be considered desirable in the interests of cricket and necessary for the benefit of scorers in particular.

Those remaining are:

To improve the standards of cricket scoring.

To co-operate and cultivate good relations with all bodies associated with cricket, for the betterment of the game.

To promote the social affairs of the membership.

So, the velvet glove remains, but the iron fist has gone and after a four-year semi-serious attempt at being a professional organisation, the ACCS has reverted to being a luncheon club committed to improving scoring skills and bonding with other cricket organisations.

The opposition to unionisation is irrational, if understandable. Trade unions have not on the whole had a favourable press and there are many who, remembering the pre-Thatcher excesses, still regard them as in *1066 and All That* terms as 'a bad thing', but the Professional Cricketers' Association exhibited no such compunction about following the Professional Footballers' Association into unionisation and ancillary associations such as the Association of Premier League and Football League Referees and Linesmen and the Stable Lads Association are happily unionised. Indeed, recent trends in industrial relations have seen the rise of white collar and professional unions as other sportsmen, university teachers and doctors have followed paths previously considered to be the province of manual and blue collar workers.

Relations between the Cricketers' Association and the TCCB/ECB have generally been amicable and it may well be that the paraphernalia of procedure agreements, minimum wages and collective bargaining may be a better basis for partnership between scorers and the ECB than the polarisation and mushroom style of management (kept in the dark and fed on crap) that has resulted from the summer of discontent. Industrial muscle has in recent times been demonstrated by baseball players in the USA, football referees in Spain and cricketers in Australia. So there would be nothing unusual or unprecedented if the scorers decided that they wished to become a trade union.

The fact that they have chosen for the time being not to do so is perhaps a reflection on the balance of the membership rather than the validity of the cause. Unlike the Cricketers' Association, the membership of which is restricted to current players only, former scorers usually become honorary life members of ACCS with full voting rights and a number of current county cricket scorers eligible for membership have declined to join or withdrawn from the Association on the grounds of its ineffectiveness. Additionally, attitudes die hard and the acceptance of scoring as a 'proper job' rather than something done by former pros and old retainers for pin money is one which will come through evolution rather than revolution. Thus, while scorers continue to whinge about pay, conditions and lack of consultation, it may be a while before they have the constitution and the will to do something about it.

An ironic twist in the tail of the tale of the ACCS's flirtation with and rejection of trade unionism is that, for World Cup scoring appointments in 1999, its officers were involved in discussions with the ECB and then adopted what opponents of militant trade unionism would see as one of its most pernicious restrictive practices, the pre-entry closed shop. The Association publicised the appointments among its membership only and processed the applications. Maybe it did not matter. Perhaps there would not have been too much competition from non-members when a pay deal of zero had been 'negotiated'.

Having emasculated itself of its powers of negotiating on status and pay, the ACCS is now in no position to act on behalf of its members to ensure recent legislation on working time and the national minimum wage is implemented. It would have been possible to do this in a totally civilised and non-contentious way by reminding the ECB of the legal position and gently suggesting that the Board enquire of its constituent bodies whether they are operating within the law. As it is, those scorers who wish to avail themselves of their new rights will be left to negotiate with their employers on an individual basis and the continuation of the 'divide and rule' ethos will be facilitated.

Compared with the maturity of other professional associations in the world of sport, the ACCS is still in its infancy. It seems the baby has been thrown out with the bathwater and it may now take a few years and a few new appointments before they begin to emulate the professionalism of the PCA which, having been largely ignored in the non-implemenation of the MacLaurin recommendations relating to first-class cricket, is now flexing a bit of industrial muscle and looking for a larger stake in the running of the game.

According to the Institute of Management:

> A professional is someone who justifiably claims to provide special knowledge and skills of value to society and accepts the duties entailed by that claim, including: the attainment and maintenance of high standards of education, training and practical judgment; honouring the special trust placed by customers, suppliers, employers and the general public.

Mutatis mutandis that must surely be a legitimate aim of those who play sport for a living and those who provide an ancillary service as officials. There is no inherent contradiction between those objectives and acting as a pressure group (trade union even, although probably not with a militant tendency) to maintain and improve professional standards.

There is, however, currently dissent within the ACCS, acrimony between the ACCS and ECB and a real danger of reversion to the polarisation of attitudes, to the amateur/professional, master/servant, milord/serf relationships that characterised the earlier part of this study and from which sport and society in general have now all but extricated themselves.

Meanwhile, the ACCS has now shot itself in the foot and in its emasculated form remains little more than a social organisation with a commitment to improving scoring standards. Such negotiating power as it had has been surrendered, it has left itself incapable of mounting a serious challenge to the Board and for the foreseeable future Malcolm Ashton is likely to remain scorer to the senior England side overseas.

With one minor exception, Ashton himself has preserved a quiet professional dignity throughout. A letter to the Editor of *The Cricketer International* accused me of inaccuracy in my reference to the appointment of a non-member of ACCS as England overseas scorer. He was, he maintained a member, having joined during the Trent Bridge Test Match. That was in August 1997. I was writing of events some two years before that. (13) That apart, he has clearly created a favourable impression, came across as a congenial, clubable, character during a spot on *Test Match Special* during a rain break in the Trinidad Test match (14) and received favourable mentions in dispatches as an efficient and effective member of the support team. (15)

Towards the end of the 1997 season, I was asked by a Test umpire what difference I thought unionisation might make. I ventured the opinion that it might mean that the Board would listen. Crystallising the relationship between the Board and and its umpires and the pecking order of umpires and scorers, he replied: 'They don't listen to *us*. You lot have no chance.'

I hope he was over-pessimistic, but the response to the MacLaurin report suggests that he was not. Around 75 per cent of members of the Cricketers' Association were in favour of changes to the current structure more radical than those which eventually emerged but their views were disregarded. A county captain and Test cricketer has expressed the view to me that 'we are all slaves to the system' and I have heard members say that the players are 'only employees' and therefore have no voice on how cricket is run. That remains the prerogative of county members. The ECB as the governing body of the game traces its descent to MCC which ran the game only a generation or so ago. Within those 30 years society's attitudes have changed and social and class barriers have become so obscure as to be almost non-existent. Flatter managerial hierarchies and employee consultation are now the norm and attempts will be made by players, umpires and scorers to look to its twenty-first century-future rather than an antecedent whose recent prevarication about admitting women places its social attitudes firmly in the nineteenth.

So, where do we go from here? It would be presumptuous of me to predict what players and umpires might do, but whether or not the new broom of the ECB turns out to be the same broom with a different handle and whether it is willing to try and re-establish harmonious relationships with its scorers remains to be seen. In the meantime, scoring is on its way to becoming a profession, supported by training and qualifications, but that process is not complete. Unlike the other professionals associated with cricket – players, umpires, physiotherapists, groundsmen – scorers are not in a position to influence the game, except in so far as the background information they provide might influence strategy and tactics.

They are there to provide a professional service firstly to those involved in a particular match whether as players, officials or spectators and secondly to those with a less direct interest, newspaper readers, statisticians and Internet surfers. The detail required by the former group is increasing and likely to be supplied in ever more sophisticated ways through linked, computerised scoreboards and scorecards and the information technology revolution is likely to increase the number of those taking an interest at one remove. Both the quality and quantity of data are increasing and the scorer cannot help but be directly involved in the generation and transmission of this information. The notchers, the telegraph, Mr Pratt's scorecards, Sam Deards's scoreboards have all been left some way back along the road, but, whether or not travelling hopefully is better than arriving, there is still work to be done before we arrive at the new Jerusalem where relations between the bodies associated with cricket will be harmonious and all the technology will be working.

Appendix A

1907	Second board at Melbourne
1911	Adelaide scoreboard
1924	New scoreboard at Sydney
1927	First radio broadcast
1930	Johnnie Walker scoreboards
1938	First television broadcast
1951	Detailed board at Trent Bridge
1953	Association of Cricket Umpires founded
1966	Frindall scoring system
1971	Linear scoring used in county cricket
1973	Association of Cricket Statisticians founded
1982	First electronic scoreboard at Melbourne
1987	Deloitte's ratings launched
1991	'Broadsystem' and Cricketscene
1992	Boxill scoring system
1993	P A Cricket Record
	Association of County Cricket Scorers founded
	'Cricinfo' on Internet
1994	Second electronic scoreboard at Melbourne
1997	Duckworth–Lewis method introduced
	Scorers' strike threatened
	ACCS decline opportunity to become trade union
1999	ACCS appoint scorers (unpaid) to World Cup teams
2005?	Networked scorebooks, scorecards and scoreboards

Appendix B

DUCKWORTH–LEWIS – AN EXPLANATION

The 'Duckworth–Lewis Method' is a system for calculating revised targets in rain-affected limited overs matches. Based on information for several hundred such matches, it takes account of the run-scoring resources (in other words, overs and wickets) available to each side.

The method ensures that an advantage gained before a break for weather is retained after it. It is therefore superior to other methods such as 'faster scoring rate' which favours the team batting second and 'most productive overs' which gives an advantage to the team batting first and made a farce of the 1992 World Cup.

Two simplified examples demonstrate how the method works:

(1) Chasing a score of 250 in 50 overs, a team has scored 125 for 3 after 25 overs when its innings is interrupted and 10 overs are lost to rain. The lost overs represent 15 per cent of the run-scoring resources of the innings, so the batting side now need 85 per cent of 250 (212.5) to match their oponents' score – or, more realistically, 213 to win the match. One fewer, in this case 212 is, from 1999, regarded as a tie.

(2) If the first innings is shortened and the redistribution of the remaining overs results in the team batting last having more resources than the team batting first, the balance is adjusted by reference to the average first innings score in 50-over matches, which is 225. Thus, if the innings of the team batting first ends with the score on 200 for 5 after 35 uninterrupted overs of a 50-over match, then, if their opponents were also allocated 35 overs, they would need 244 to win.

The target in the second example is more logical than it might at first appear, since a team knowing it has only 35 overs available would expect to score more in those 35 overs than it would in the first 35 overs of a 50-over innings.

If there is more than one interruption, the target is recalculated after each and, if there is bad weather around, the scoreboard will show by a plus or minus figure at the end of each over the position of the batting side in relation to what the Duckworth–Lewis target would be if the match were abandoned at that stage.

Appendix C

RESOLUTION OF EXTRAORDINARY GENERAL MEETING OF THE ASSOCIATION OF COUNTY CRICKET SCORERS

Mindful of the duplicity with which the England and Wales Cricket Board and its predecessor have treated the appointment of Scorer to England touring sides and particularly resentful of

> (a) the appointment for a third consecutive winter of a scorer from outside the County circuit;
> and
> (b) the manner in which that appointment has been made and announced,

this Association, having considered the possibility of industrial action, but sharing the wish of the ECB for increased professionalism in the provision of scoring services,

RESOLVES

to urge the Board to appoint County Scorers for all England overseas tours, including 'A' and Under 19 tours.

Derby, 28 July 1997

Notes

Chapter 1

(1) Neville Cardus *English Cricket* (1945) p9
(2) Frank Birbalsingh *The Rise of West Indian Cricket from Colony to Nation* (1996) *passim*
(3) *Wisden Cricketers' Almanack* (1963) p138
(4) C.L.R. James *Beyond A Boundary* (1969) p116
(5) MCC Committee minutes 18 May 1846
(6) *Colliers Encyclopedia* (1990) pp652–3
(7) Christopher Brookes *English Cricket* (1978) p7
(8) A. Steel *The Receipt of the Exchequer 1377–1485* (1954) Ch 1, quoted in G.R. Elton The Tudor Constitution (1962) p128
(9) Rev. James Pycroft *The Cricket Field* (1851), edited by F.S. Ashley-Cooper (1922) p91
(10) J. Burnby *The Kentish Cricketer* (1773)
(11) R.S. Rait Kerr *The Laws of Cricket: Their History and Growth* (1950) p25
(12) William Goldwin *In Certamen Pilae, Anglice, A Cricket Match, Musae Juveniles* (1706) p10, translated by H.A. Perry *Etoniana* (30 Dec 1922) pp481-3, and P.F. Thomas *Early Cricket* (1923)
(13) Quoted in V. Sackville West *Knole and the Sackvilles* (1922)
(14) Robin Simon and Alastair Smart *Art of Cricket* (1983) p87
(15) Rowland Bowen *Cricket: A History of its Growth and Development throughout the World* (1970) p57
(16) Gerald Brodribb *Next Man In: A Survey of Cricket Laws and Customs* (1952, updated 1985 and 1995) p26
(17) Marcus Williams and Gordon Phillips *Wisden Book of Cricket Memorabilia* (1990) p221
(18) Quoted by Marshall Lee in *The Scorer* no 5 spring 1995

Chapter 2

(1) Centre for Kentish Studies, Maidstone U269 F14
(2) Bowen *Cricket: A History of its Growth* p56
(3) Marshall Lee 'Run Outs Anonymous', *The Scorer* no 5 spring 1995
(4) Centre for Kentish Studies U24 F44
(5) Ibid U310 F45
(6) Stephen Green *Some Cricket Records (Archives Volume XVIII no 80 1988)* pp192–3

(7) Robert Brooke and Peter Matthews *Cricket Firsts* (1988) p130

(8) Alfred D. Taylor *Annals of Lord's and History of the MCC* (1903) p56

(9) Lillywhite's *Scores and Biographies of Celebrated Cricketers* (1862) Vol. 1 p57

(10) Public Record Office COPY/3/6

(11) Pycroft *The Cricket Field* p91

(12) Peter Wynne-Thomas 'The Scorebooks at Trent Bridge', *The Scorer* no 6 summer 1995

(13) *The Cricket Statistician* summer 1995

(14) Surrey County Record Office, Woking 2042/8/1-12

(15) Bill Frindall *Wisden Book of Test Cricket* (1977) p16

(16) Charles Box *The English Game of Cricket* (1877) pp399 ff

CHAPTER 3

(1) Hampshire County Record Office, Winchester 10M89

(2) Lonsdale Library of Sports, Games and Pastimes: *Cricket* (1930) p163

(3) *Barclay's World of Cricket (1987)* edited by E. W. Swanton pp654–7

(4) Association of Cricket Umpires and Scorers *Tom Smith's Cricket Umpiring and Scoring* (1996) p219

(5) W.H. Ferguson *Mr Cricket* (1957) pp56–7

(6) Ibid pp13–14

(7) W.A. Bettesworth *The Walkers of Southgate* (1900) p299

(8) Derek Hibbs *Cricket Scoring* (1994) p70

(9) Bill Frindall *Ten Tests for England: Scorebook and Journal 1988* (1989) pp22–8

(10) Ferguson *Mr Cricket* pp56–7

(11) *Wisden Cricketers' Almanack 1958* p959

(12) Brian Johnston and Roy Webber *Armchair Cricket* (1957) pp37–49

(13) Richard Streeton *P.G.H. Fender A Biography* (1981) p87

(14) Douglas Jardine *In Quest of the Ashes* pp235–247

(15) Assuming two run penalty for a no ball is in operation: otherwise, under the Laws of Cricket, it's 11

CHAPTER 4

(1) Nigel Mitson *Cricket World* November 1993 p7

(2) Ian Leach in interview with Eleanor Oldroyd on *Test Match Special* BBC Radio 5, 22 February 1993

(3) Matthew Engel *The Guardian* 27 May 1993

(4) *Cricket World* July 1993 p4

(5) *Wisden 1994* p49

(6) Ibid p48

(7) John Thicknesse *Woolmer gives England glimpse of the future, Evening Standard* 27 February 1996

CHAPTER 5

(1) Don Oslear with Don Mosey *Wisden Book of Cricket Laws* (1993) p26

(2) Lillywhite's *Scores and Biographies* Vol. 1 p57

(3) Dr Vasant Naik *When Scorers Differ! The Scorer* no 5 spring 1995

(4) Ferguson *Mr Cricket* p20

(5) Keith Booth *Atherton's Progress* (1996) pp40 & 247

(6) *Playfair Cricket Annual 1995* p25

(7) *The Cricketer International* December 1998 and subsequent correspondence January 1999

CHAPTER 6

(1) Teresa McLean *The Men in White Coats* (1987) p44

(2) Ibid p95

(3) W.G. Grace *Cricket* (1891) p15

(4) MCC minutes 18 March 1846

(5) Lillywhite's *Scores and Biographies* Vol. 1 p2

(6) Taylor *Annals of Lord's* p101

(7) Brooke and Matthews *Cricket Firsts* p129

(8) Kent County Cricket Club archive Centre for Kentish Studies Ch 75

(9) W. Robson *Twentieth Century Britain* (1983) p165

(10) Ferguson *Mr Cricket* p15

(11) Ibid p19

(12) Ibid pp58–59

(13) SCRO 2042/4/1

(14) Ric Sissons *The Players: A Social History of the Professional Cricketer* (1988) p49

(15) Ibid pp148–50

(16) Ibid p95

(17) Irving Rosenwater *A Note on County Scorers, Journal of the Cricket Society* Vol. 16 no 4 spring 1994

(18) Hampshire County Cricket Club accounts Hampshire County Record Office 10M89/65

(19) Nick Yapp *A History of the Foster's Oval* (1990) p128

(20) Sissons *The Players* p206

(21) *The Times* 9 June 1997

(22) Bill Frindall *Limited Overs International Cricket: The Complete Record* Preface pviii

CHAPTER 7

(1) Pycroft *The Cricket Field* pp91–2

CHAPTER 8

(1) Taylor *Annals of Lords* p110

(2) Brodribb *Next Man In* p28

(3) *The Australians in England 1882* (reprinted from *Bell's Life*)

(4) *Cricket: A Weekly Record of the Game* 16 September 1886 p421

(5) Surrey County Cricket Club minutes SCRO. 2042/1/5

(6) R. Abel in front of scoreboard showing his record 357*

(7) Ground Committee minutes SCRO. 2042/4/1

(8) David Hopps *An Alternative Five* Wisden 1995 p54

(9) Yapp *A History of the Foster's Oval* p19

(10) *Cricket* Vol. 17 14 July 1898 p275

(11) Surrey County Cricket Club minutes SCRO. 2042/1/7

(12) Ground Committee minutes SCRO 2042/4/2

(13) *The Times* 12 March 1953

(14) D.R. Seagrave *The Parish of Harlow in the Nineteenth Century*

(15) George Taylor *The Archive Photograph Series: Harlow* (1995)

(16) Kent County Cricket Club Archive Centre for Kentish Studies Ch 75

(17) 'Johnnie Walker' Still Scoring: *Wine and Spirit Trade Record* 14 July 1930 and *DCL Gazette* July 1930

(18) A. Scott 'Watching the Tests from the Seaside' *The Cricketer* 30 June 1934

CHAPTER 9

(1) Quoted in W.J. Lewis *The Language of Cricket* (1934) p228

(2) Maurice Golesworthy *Encyclopedia of Cricket* (6th Edition 1976) p168

(3) Jack Pollard *Complete Illustrated History of Australian Cricket* (1992) p140

(4) Giles Walkley 'High over Long Off', *The Adelaide Review* February and March 1995

(5) P.F. Warner *How we Recovered the Ashes* (1904) p60

(6) Pollard *Complete Illustrated History of Australian Cricket*

(7) Walkley *High over Long Off*

(8) Ibid

(9) Ian Wooldridge *The Daily Mail* 21 February 1997
(10) Barbi Wills 'Transvaal's Computerised Scoreboard', *The Scorer* no 4
     winter 1994

CHAPTER 10

(1) Brodribb *Next Man In* p27
(2) MCC minutes 19 May 1886
(3) Golesworthy *Encyclopedia of Cricket* p168
(4) Altham *Dates in Cricket History* p179
(5) Brooke and Matthews *Cricket Firsts* p168
(6) Williams and Phillips *Wisden Book of Cricket Memorabilia* p221
(7) From the Roger Mann collection, illustrated in
     The Illustrated History of County Cricket (1992) p14
(8) Williams and Phillips *Wisden Book of Cricket Memorabilia* p221
(9) Altham *Dates in Cricket History* p180
(10) Midwinter *The Illustrated History of County Cricket* p46
(11) Brodribb *Next Man In* pp32–3
(12) *Lonsdale Library* p165
(13) Surrey County Cricket Club minutes SCRO. 2042/1/3
(14) Ibid Agenda Book SCRO. 2074
(15) Ibid minutes SCRO. 2042/1/7
(16) Ibid minutes SCRO. 2042/4/2
(17) *Cricket* 28 January 1897
(18) Geoffrey Moorhouse *Lord's* (1983) p110
(19) Surrey C C C minutes SCRO. 2042/1/13
(20) Williams and Phillips *Wisden Book of Cricket Memorabilia* pp207 and 222
(21) Surrey C C C Agenda Book SCRO. 2074
(22) MCC Collection, Lord's
(23) Rt Hon. Lord Alverstone and C.W. Alcock *Surrey Cricket: Its History and
     Associations* (1902) p244

CHAPTER 11

(1) Brobribb *Next Man In* p32
(2) Statistics: The History of Statistical Method in *International
     Encyclopedia of the Social Sciences* ed: David L Sills (1968) Vol. 15 pp226–7
(3) David & Julia Jary *Dictionary of Sociology* (1991) p654
(4) Bettesworth *The Walkers of Southgate* p245
(5) Simon Rae *W.G. Grace: A Life* (1998) Illustration 9, following p172
(6) *The Cricketer International* June 1996 and December 1996 p45

(7) Alan Pavelin 'A life table approach to batting averages', *The Actuary* October 1994

(8) Simon Wilde 'Statisticians take issue with Wisden', *The Times* 1 April 1995 p40

(9) Michael Pearce 'The Surrey Statistics Group', *Surrey CCC Yearbook* 1996 p54

(10) *The Cricket Statistician* winter 1996

(11) *The Cricketer International* March 1997

CHAPTER 12

(1) Brodribb *Next Man In* p32

(2) Ted Lester *The Scorer* no 7 autumn 1995

(3) Kent County Cricket Club Archive Centre for Kentish Studies Ch 75

(4) Theo Braganza *The Scorer* no 7 autumn 1995

(5) Robert Brooke *The Cricket Statistician* spring 1997 no 97

(6) David Frith *The Scorer* no 1 spring 1994

(7) Jack Bannister Ibid

(8) *The Guardian* 19 July 1997

(9) *The Daily Telegraph* 19 July 1997

(10) *Wisden* 1998 p1,417

(11) *Wisden* 1967 p890

(12) *Wisden* 1996 p1,011

(13) *The Cricketer International* Letters September and October 1997

(14) *Test Match Special* 16 February 1998

(15) Alan Lee 'England's new support system geared to produce harmony', *The Times* 5 March 1998

Illustrations

1. W.R. Coates – A Cricket Match (c1760) [Tate Gallery]

2. Duke of Dorset's XI v Wrotham 31 August 1769 [by permission of Lord Sackville and the Centre for Kentish Studies (U269 F14)]

3. Scoresheet of first Test Match played in England: England v Australia at The Oval 6,7 & 8 September 1880 [Surrey County Cricket Club]

4. Australia's second innings scoresheet in traditional format, from England v Australia at The Oval August 1997 [Surrey County Cricket Club]

5. Charles Box's Bowling Analysis Example 1877

6. Burwood v Surrey Club and Ground at Hersham 11 August 1858 [Surrey C C C]

7. England's 46 all out at Port of Spain, Trinidad 29 & 30 March 1994 [Bill Frindall]

8. Australia's second innings scoresheet in linear form from England v Australia at The Oval August 1997 [Surrey County Cricket Club]

9. James Lillywhite's Telegraph 1872

10. Deakin's Patent Telegraph 1883

11. Paget's Patent Scorer 1886

12. Deards Scoreboard 1902

13. Deards scoreboard at Harlow Cricket Club – now derelict [Author's collection]

14. Johnnie Walker Scoreboard 1930 in Brighton [United Distillers]

15. Selection of contemporary scoreboards [Author's collection]

16. Holmes & Sutcliffe (1932) break Brown & Tunnicliffe's 1898 record [Yorkshire County Cricket Club]

17. Melbourne scoreboard 1926, Victoria v New South Wales [MCG Collection]

18. Adelaide scoreboard 1893, South Australia v New South Wales [MCG Collection]

19. Current Adelaide scoreboard 1987 [Adelaide Oval Museum]

20. Hambledon v England at Sevenoaks Vine 1773 [Sevenoaks Vine C C]

21. Canada v Philadelphia 15 September 1875 [Lord's]

22. Eton College averages 1852 [Eton College]

Bibliography

ABC Australian Cricket Almanack, Queen Anne Press
Allan's Australian Cricket Annual, McPherson
Altham, H.S. and Swanton, E.W. *A History of Cricket*, Allen and Unwin, 1962
Alverstone, Rt Hon. Lord and Alcock, C.W. *Surrey Cricket: Its History and Associations*, Longman, 1902
Association of Cricket Umpires and Scorers *Tom Smith's Cricket Umpiring and Scoring*, Weidenfeld and Nicholson, 1996
The Australians in England 1882 (reprinted from *Bell's Life*)
Barclay's World of Cricket edited by E.W. Swanton, Collins Willow 1987
Bentley, Henry *A Correct Account of All the Cricket Matches Played by the Marylebone Club*, T. Traveller, 1823
Bettesworth, W.A. *The Walkers of Southgate*, Methuen, 1900
Birbalsingh, Frank *The Rise of West Indian Cricket from Colony to Nation*, Hansib, St John's, Antigua, 1996
Booth, Keith *Atherton's Progress*, Clifford Frost, 1996
Bowen, Rowland *Cricket: A History of its Growth and Development throughout the World*, Eyre and Spottiswoode, 1970
Box, Charles *The English Game of Cricket*, 'The Field', 1877
Brodribb, Gerald *Next Man In: A Survey of Cricket's Laws and Customs*, Putman, 1952 and Souvenir Press (updated 1995)
Brooke, Robert and Matthews, Peter *Cricket Firsts*, Guinness, 1988
Brookes, Christopher *English Cricket*, Weidenfeld and Nicolson, 1978
Cardus, Neville *English Cricket*, Collins, 1945
The Cricketer (later *The Cricketer International*)
Elton, G.R. *The Tudor Constitution*, Cambridge University Press, 1962
Ferguson, W.H. *Mr Cricket*, Kaye, 1957
Frindall, Bill *Limited Overs International Cricket: The Complete Record*, Headline, 1997
Frindall, Bill *Ten Tests for England: Scorebook and Journal for 1988*, Columbus, 1989
Frindall, Bill *Wisden Book of Test Cricket*, Macdonald and Jane's, 1977
Golesworthy, *Encyclopedia of Cricket* (6th Edition), Robert Hale, 1976
Goldwin, William *In Certamen Pilae, Anglice, A Cricket Match*, Baldwin, 1706
Grace, W.G. *Cricket*, Arrowsmith, 1891
Hibbs, Derek *Cricket Scoring*, Quacks Books, 1994
James, C.L.R. *Beyond a Boundary*, Hutchinson, 1969
Jardine, Douglas *In Quest of the Ashes*, Hutchinson, 1933 and Orbis, 1984
Jary, David & Julia *Dictionary of Sociology*, HarperCollins, 1991
Johnston, Brian and Webber, Roy *Armchair Cricket*, BBC, 1957
Johnston, Brian *Armchair Cricket*, BBC, 1975
Lewis, W.J. *The Language of Cricket*, Oxford University Press, 1934
Lillywhite's *Guide to Cricketers, Cricketers' Companion* and *Cricketers' Annual* 1849–1900

Lillywhite's Scores and Biographies of Celebrated Cricketers (Volumes 1–15) 1862–1925

Lonsdale Library of Sports, Games and Pastimes, ed Earl of Lonsdale and Eric Parker, Seeley, Service & Co. Ltd, 1930

McLean, Teresa *The Men in White Coats*, Stanley Paul, 1987

Midwinter, Eric *The Illustrated History of County Cricket*, Kingswood Press 1992

Moorhouse, Geoffrey *Lord's*, Hodder and Stoughton, 1983

Oslear, Don with Don Mosey *Wisden Book of Cricket Laws*, Stanley Paul, 1993

Playfair Cricket Annual

Pollard, Jack *Complete Illustrated History of Australian Cricket*, Pelham Books,1992

Pycroft, Rev. James *The Cricket Field*, Longmans, 1851, edited by F.S. Ashley-Cooper, St James' Press, 1922

Rae Simon *W.G. Grace: A Life*, Faber and Faber, 1998

Rait Kerr, R.S. *Cricket Umpiring and Scoring*, Phoenix House, 1957

Rait Kerr, R.S. *The Laws of Cricket: Their History and Growth*, Longman 1950

Robson, W *Twentieth Century Britain*, Oxford University Press, 1983

Ross, Gordon *The Surrey Story*, Stanley Paul, 1957

The Scorer (1994–1998) ed Michael R.L.W. Ayers

Simon, Robin and Smart, Alastair *Art of Cricket*, Martin Secker and Warburg, 1983

Sissons, Ric *The Players: A Social History of the Professional Cricketer*, Kingswood Press, 1988

Steel, A *The Receipt of the Exchequer 1377–1485*, 1954

Streeton, Richard *P.G.H. Fender: A Biography*, Faber and Faber, 1981

Taylor, Alfred D. *Annals of Lord's and History of the M.C.C.*, Arrowsmith, 1903

Taylor, George *The Archive Photograph Series: Harlow*, Chalford Publishing Company, 1995

Warner, P.F. *How we Recovered the Ashes*, Chapman and Hall, 1904

Williams, Marcus and Phillips, Gordon *Wisden Book of Cricket Memorabilia*, Lennard, 1990

Wisden Cricketers' Almanack

Wright, Graeme *Betrayal, The Struggle for Cricket's Soul*, Witherby, 1994

Wrigley, Arthur *The Book of Test Cricket 1876–1964*, Epworth Press, 1965

Yapp, Nick *A History of the Foster's Oval*, Pelham Books, 1990

Index